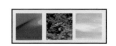

Geography of Extreme Environments

DESERTS

POLAR REGIONS

THE TROPICS

Extreme Climates

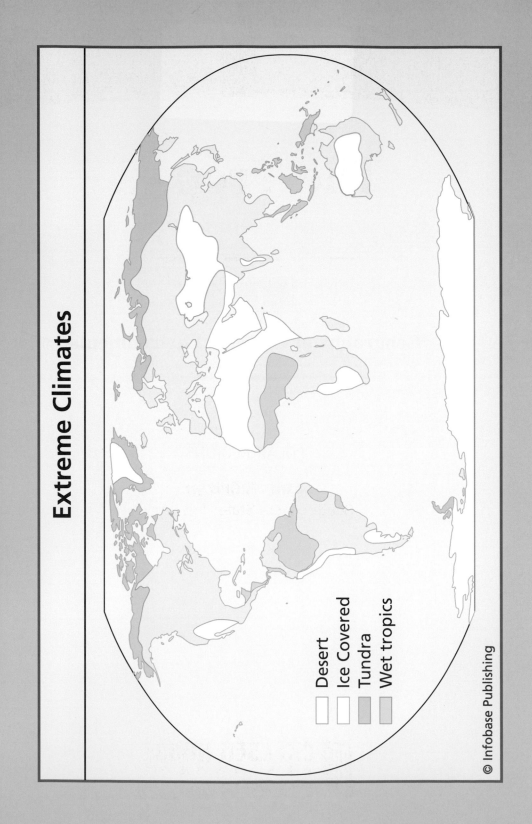

Desert
Ice Covered
Tundra
Wet tropics

The Tropics

Charles F. Gritzner
South Dakota State University

CHELSEA HOUSE
PUBLISHERS
An imprint of Infobase Publishing

FRONTIS The Polar Regions, Wet Tropics, and Deserts are highlighted on this map of the world's extreme climates.

The Tropics

Chelsea House
An imprint of Infobase Publishing
132 West 31st Street
New York, NY 10001

Library of Congress Cataloging-in-Publication Data

Gritzner, Charles F.
  The tropics / Charles F. Gritzner.
    p. cm. — (Geography of extreme environments)
  Includes bibliographical references and index.
  ISBN 0-7910-9233-X (hardcover)
1. Tropics—Juvenile literature. I. Title.
  G907.G75 2006
  910.913—dc22

Chelsea House books are available at special discounts when purchased in bulk quantities for businesses, associations, institutions, or sales promotions. Please call our Special Sales Department in New York at (212) 967-8800 or (800) 322-8755.

You can find Chelsea House on the World Wide Web at http://www.chelseahouse.com

Series design by Keith Trego
Cover design by Ben Peterson

Printed in the United States of America

Bang KT 10 9 8 7 6 5 4 3 2 1

This book is printed on acid-free paper.

All links and Web addresses were checked and verified to be correct at the time of publication. Because of the dynamic nature of the Web, some addresses and links may have changed since publication and may no longer be valid.

Contents

Introducing the Wet Tropical Realm

The Wet Tropics: Few of Earth's environments can match the hot, steamy equatorial region for evoking strong emotions, presenting sharp contrasts, or being more shrouded in mystery and myth. This is a chief geographic characteristic of the world's extreme environments: the Arctic, Desert, and Wet Tropical lands. We may be repelled by them, but at the same time, we are fascinated by their extreme and often exotic conditions. Certainly this is true of the Wet Tropics, an environment defined on the basis of its high temperature and abundant year-round rainfall.

From the dawn of human history—believed by scientists to have begun in the equatorial tropics of East Africa—humans have been and continue to be tropical animals. As such, we are very poorly adapted *biologically* to the cold. Culture is humankind's adaptive mechanism. Our knowledge, tools, and skills, rather than our bodies, made it possible to slip the bonds of nature's grip and move into nontropical lands. It is ironic that what was once our biological homeland has more recently been described in such terms as *White Man's Grave* and *Green Hell*. Early Greek scholars even believed that human life could not survive in what they called the "torrid zone."

To nineteenth-century Europeans, Africa was the "Dark Continent." In South America, one early explorer, after traveling in the Orinoco River Basin, is believed to have stated, "He who travels the Orinoco, either dies or comes back loco [crazy]." In some instances, such perceptions hold a kernel of truth. Viewed through the lens of geography, however, more positive images emerge as one comes to better know and understand this fascinating environment.

Today, at least parts of the region once feared as a "White Man's Grave" have become a vacationer's paradise. The tropics offer the lure of "sun, sand, and surf," where one can enjoy the region's warm tropical breezes, swaying palms, azure seas, and exotic cultures. In many locations, the tropical rain forest once viewed as a "Green Hell" has now become a "verdant tropical paradise" that draws thousands of ecotourists. Some tropical locations, such as South America's Amazon River Basin and Africa's Congo River Basin, support very low population densities. Elsewhere, however, similar tropical lands are home to some of the world's densest populations. In fact, 5 of the world's 10 most populated countries lie either partly or entirely in the tropics. From our midlatitude vantage point, when we look toward the tropics, we stereotypically see widespread poverty and low levels of cultural attainment. Historically, however, the tropics were home to many, if not most, early advanced civilizations. Today, people living in places such as Hawaii, Barbados, and Singapore enjoy the incomes and living standards of those living in the developed world.

The tropics, as you can see, are many things to many people. Several perceptions held by outsiders are valid (yes, there are bugs!), yet exceptions make it hazardous to generalize about the region. Throughout this book, attention is repeatedly focused on explaining such contrasting perspectives. Most of

Many vacationers flock to the tropics to relax on its many beaches. Pictured here is the world-renowned Ipanema Beach in Rio de Janeiro, Brazil.

the remarkable contrasts that exist from place to place within the Wet Tropical realm can be easily explained geographically. Answers often lie in the location or conditions of the natural environment; in other instances, explanations are found in the history of the places and culture (way of life) of the people who inhabit them.

HOW ARE "TROPICS" DEFINED?

When you think of "tropical lands," what comes to mind? Do you think of places like the parched desert region of the American Southwest? What about San Francisco, California, or, for that matter, much of Ireland? Climatologists (scientists who study average conditions of weather) use many different elements to identify climatic regions. By some systems, the places just mentioned would be classified as tropical. Usually, when we think of a tropical land's conditions, *hot*, *humid*, *rainy*, and *monotonous* are words that immediately come to mind. For the purposes of this book, those four traits are appropriate. Most climatic classification systems, though, use one or more of the following five criteria in defining "tropics":

1. **Latitudinal position.** One system, traced back more than 2,000 years to the ancient Greeks, uses latitudinal position on Earth's surface. According to this tradition, the tropics are those lands lying in a belt located between the Tropic of Cancer (23 1/2 degrees north latitude) and the Tropic of Capricorn (23 1/2 degrees south latitude). This system has many problems. As you will learn in Chapter 2, various factors combine to determine a particular location's weather and climate. For example, both permanently freezing temperatures and mountain glaciers can be found near the equator in South America, Africa, and Indonesia.

2. **Lack of distinct seasons contributing to extreme monotony.** This definition also is flawed. There are no distinct seasons in the heart of Antarctica, yet that frigid continent certainly is not tropical. In addition, some tropical lands, such as portions of India, have pronounced wet and dry seasons.

3. **Annual temperature range of 12°F (7°C) or less.** Using this definition, many locations on the U.S. West Coast, such as San Francisco, and coastal southwestern England and Ireland would be classified as tropical.

4. **Frost never occurs.** Several areas of the world far removed from the tropics never experience freezing conditions. Almost always, this is because they are located along a coast bathed by a warm ocean current.

5. **All months' average temperatures greater than 65°F (17°C).** Most geographers and climatologists define "tropics" as those locations where the average temperature of all months is greater than 65°F (17°C). In those locations

where the coldest monthly temperature average is 65°F or warmer, most of the other four conditions also prevail.

In this book, however, we need not be greatly concerned about a precise definition of or boundary to our region. What is important is that readers think in terms of a *general* location and *general* atmospheric and other environmental conditions. In addition, it is important to realize that tropical conditions present certain problems and also prospects for human adaptation and use of land and resources. Many of the world's deserts fall within one or more of the foregoing definitions. Tropical Deserts are not considered in this book. (Deserts are, however, one of the three "Extreme Environments" covered in this geography series.) Many lands with tropical temperatures experience sharp differences in seasonal precipitation. These "Wet and Dry Tropical" and "Monsoon Tropical" regions will be discussed only where appropriate in the context of Wet Tropical lands and peoples.

The region as arbitrarily defined for purposes of this book includes the following characteristics: (1) hot and humid throughout the year; (2) little seasonal variation in temperature or precipitation, contributing to extreme monotony; (3) large amounts of annual precipitation, generally exceeding 60 inches (150 centimeters), with no period of pronounced drought; and (4) the world's highest annual average temperatures (although not the highest extreme temperatures). In other words, tropical lands are those experiencing hot, humid, rainy, and extremely monotonous conditions throughout the year. Under natural conditions, they also support a dense ("rain forest") vegetation cover and agriculture that never requires irrigation. Lands experiencing these conditions occur in equatorial South America, Africa, and Asia; they also occur because of the moderating influence of the trade winds, on the eastern sides of some land masses poleward to 20 degrees in both hemispheres.

What are tropical lands called? Surprisingly, perhaps, they go by many names. In fact, the author once conducted a survey of terminology used in different high-school-level world regional geography textbooks. To his amazement, the eight books included in the study identified this region by eight different names: Wet Tropical, Humid Tropical, Rainy Tropical, Tropical Moist, Tropical Rainy, Tropical Rain Forest, Equatorial Tropical, and Af ("A" meaning tropical and "f" meaning moist throughout the year). The author prefers Wet Tropical to describe the region discussed in this book. Other tropical lands include the bordering Wet and Dry Tropics and Monsoon Tropics, which experience a marked seasonal distribution of precipitation, and Tropical Deserts.

WHY ARE THE TROPICS IMPORTANT TO US?

To a geographer, all places are important simply because they are there. About places and their conditions, geographers generally ask, "*What* is *where*, *why* is it there, and *why* should we *care*?" This is a question that you will want to keep in mind as you learn about the Wet Tropics and the region's varied physical, historical, and cultural conditions. In regard to the *care* portion of the question, how many agricultural products do you and your family and friends consume that are tropical in origin? Have you enjoyed a banana, pineapple, coconut, or some exotic fruit juice recently? Do you drink coffee or tea, or put sugar (from sugarcane) in your drinks, or on your cereal? How many rubber products can you think of, including, of course, the tires on cars and bicycles? How many products do you have that are made from aluminum? These are just some of many tropical products that we enjoy on a regular basis.

The importance of tropical lands goes deeper, however. In terms of physical geography, the Wet Tropics are a gigantic "engine" that influences weather and climate across the globe. El Niño, a shift in the temperature of equatorial oceanic water off the coast of equatorial Ecuador, wreaks havoc on weather patterns throughout much of the world. Ocean currents transport warm tropical water poleward in both

Coffee is one of the most important agricultural products grown in the Wet Tropics region. Here, a worker harvests Kona Coffee beans, which are cultivated on the slopes of Mount Hualalai and Mauna Loa on the island of Hawaii.

hemispheres. In North America and Europe, west coastal areas are much warmer than they would be without the gift of tropical warmth. Tropical rain forests act as "scrubbers" that remove carbon dioxide from the atmosphere, thereby perhaps reducing the greenhouse effect and the threat of global warming. These are just a few of the ways that the physical geography of the Wet Tropics is important for us all.

The Wet Tropics are important for many cultural reasons as well. Blacks, for example, represent about 13 percent of the American population. Most are descendents of people brought from tropical Africa to tropical and subtropical America to toil as slaves raising tropical products. Today, an estimated 11 million undocumented foreigners are living and working in the United States, most of whom have come from impoverished tropical or subtropical countries. Also, many of today's political hot spots are in the tropics.

Of greatest significance may be the fact that many tropical lands are still in the process of undergoing perhaps the greatest change in human history. Several centuries ago, the Industrial Revolution began to radically transform much of western Europe. Soon, industrialization, jobs and a cash economy, urban centers with factories and services, the need for literacy, and many other social and cultural changes began to transform the way people lived. These ideas spread, first to Northern America, then to Australia and New Zealand, and gradually to other areas of the world. Much of the tropical world, however, has only recently begun to become involved in this transformation. The importance of this revolution and its impact on people throughout the less-developed countries (LDCs) will be discussed in subsequent chapters.

WHERE WILL WE GO ON OUR TROPICAL JOURNEY?

In this book, you will learn about the conditions of weather and climate that make this region unique. Climate, of course, is a primary influence on ecosystems—in this case, the dense tropical rain forest, abundant wildlife, relatively infertile soils, and ample water resources. As the initial home of humankind, the tropics became the first environment to which humans adapted. Today, however, many cultures (ways of living) are found throughout the region. European influences on tropical realm peoples are relatively recent, extending back only about 500 years, and much more recent in some areas.

Almost always, contacts with midlatitude peoples have resulted in a clash of values, social patterns, means of economic survival, and other aspects of culture. By and large, the

European influence has always been extractive and exploitative. Emphasis has been on the taking of slave laborers, the harvesting of mineral and forest resources, and the development of plantations with both products and revenue benefiting midlatitude interests. Past and present aspects of the region's cultural, social, economic, and political geography will be discussed at length. Finally, we will take a brief tour of the various regions that make up the Wet Tropics and glimpse into the region's future. Turn on the air-conditioning, put on some insect repellent, and get ready to begin your visit to the extreme geographical environment of the world's Wet Tropical lands and peoples.

2

Weather and Climate of the Wet Tropics

Think of a scorching hot, muggy (humid), sultry summer day. How would you like nearly every day of your life to be just like that? This is exactly what it is like year-round in the Wet Tropics. On a typical day, clouds begin to form in mid-to late morning and by early to mid-afternoon, huge thunderheads loom overhead. The air is deathly still, with not a breath of breeze to offer relief from the stifling heat and humidity. Few people are seen moving about; even dogs and other animals seem to have vanished. You feel clammy as your clothing becomes saturated with perspiration in these sweltering conditions.

Suddenly, a bolt of lightning signals the onset of drenching afternoon thundershowers. Rain begins to fall in torrents. As quickly as it began, however, the storm passes. You notice that the temperature has dropped by as much as 5°F to 10°F (3°C to 6°C). Humidity begins to drop as well, and a cooling breeze begins to stir. As evening approaches, the sun sets rapidly and the sky darkens in

16

minutes. Temperatures begin to cool, and the sounds of evening fill the air. This is the typical weather, day after day, month after month, year after year in Wet Tropical locations. Now you know why *monotonous* is the word that perhaps best describes the region.

The conditions just described refer to daily conditions of the atmosphere, or the weather. Climate, on the other hand, refers to average weather conditions spread over a period of decades. In the Wet Tropics, the daily weather is hot and wet; therefore, so is the climate. With the possible exception of interior Antarctica, no place on Earth experiences conditions of daily weather and long-term climate that are more alike.

WHY IS THE WET TROPICAL CLIMATE SO MONOTONOUS?

The weather and climate experienced in any location is the product of a finely tuned environmental system. Specific conditions are the result of many different controls functioning together to produce an atmospheric result. Some elements, such as elevation or proximity to a large water body and prevailing winds, are constant. Others, such as duration of sunlight or the angle at which the sun's rays strike Earth's surface, however, change with the seasons in most locations. This is why those of us living in the middle latitudes experience four distinct seasons. If, on the other hand, controls remain fairly constant, as is the case in the Wet Tropics, weather conditions will experience little daily or seasonal change. A very simple example is the weather and climate experienced where most readers live. In the midlatitudes, summer months have longer daylight hours, and the sun is higher in the sky during its daily passage. The result is warm-to-hot summer days. During winter months, daylight hours are much shorter, and the sun is much lower in the sky. Its rays strike Earth's surface at a lower angle; therefore, winter days tend to be cool to cold.

In the Wet Tropics, the controls of weather and climate remain very constant. Imagine yourself on a seesaw. As you go up and down, half of the time you are above the fulcrum point (middle), and half the time below. When you reach the very top of the back-and-forth bounce, think of yourself as being at the North Pole, where the sun does not set for six months. When you are at the bottom, you are at the South Pole, and, because you are below the fulcrum, you are experiencing six months of darkness. Notice the middle of the board, though. Does it move up or down? No, it remains in the same place, moving neither upward nor downward. The same holds true at the equator with regard to the duration of sunlight. The sun always rises at 6:00 A.M. (solar time, rather than time zones) and sets at (solar) 6:00 P.M. At zero degrees latitude, the sun is also almost always vertically overhead, never straying more than 23 1/2 degrees north or south. This consistency in the 12-hour duration of sunlight and the high angle at which the sun's rays strike Earth's surface are the keys to understanding temperature in the Wet Tropics.

A region's weather and climate are the result of four separate weather elements: temperature, atmospheric pressure and winds, precipitation, and storms. Our attention now turns to a discussion of each element in terms of specific conditions and why they occur.

TEMPERATURE

Temperatures in the Wet Tropical climate offer several surprises. First, the equatorial region is not where Earth's highest absolute temperatures occur. In fact, very few Wet Tropical locations have ever recorded a temperature exceeding 100°F (40°C). For example, several spots near and even north of the Arctic Circle have experienced higher temperatures than have any locations on or near the equator. This can be easily explained. First, as long as the sun is shining, it is heating Earth's surface. The longer it shines, the more effectively it heats. At the equator, the sun is only above the horizon for 12 hours a day, in contrast to the 20 or more hours it shines at poleward latitudes. Second, during what normally would be

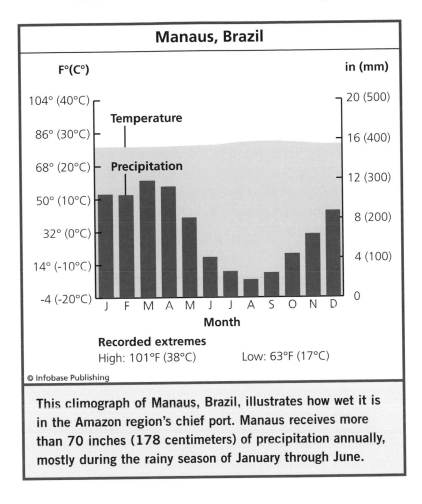

Manaus, Brazil

F°(C°)   in (mm)

104° (40°C)   20 (500)

Temperature

86° (30°C)   16 (400)

68° (20°C)   **Precipitation**   12 (300)

50° (10°C)   8 (200)

32° (0°C)

14° (-10°C)   4 (100)

-4 (-20°C)   J F M A M J J A S O N D   0

Month

Recorded extremes
High: 101°F (38°C)   Low: 63°F (17°C)

© Infobase Publishing

This climograph of Manaus, Brazil, illustrates how wet it is in the Amazon region's chief port. Manaus receives more than 70 inches (178 centimeters) of precipitation annually, mostly during the rainy season of January through June.

the hottest time of the day, when the sun is highest in the sky, cloud cover partially blocks incoming solar radiation (solar energy). These conditions combine to prevent extremely high temperatures from occurring. Third, the atmosphere is very moist, and moist air takes longer to heat than does drier air.

A second surprising condition is that daytime temperature extremes are greater than seasonal extremes in the Wet Tropics—often by a wide margin. By definition, tropical lands are areas in which no monthly temperature average falls below 65°F (18°C). In the Wet Tropics, however, most weather stations experience a mean annual temperature range between perhaps 77° to 81°F (25° to 27°C). Several locations, such as some tropical islands, experience no temperature difference whatsoever from month to month. Most locations have a 1-to 3-degree range (< 1.5°C).

The daily temperature in most Wet Tropical locations ranges from the low 70s to upper 80s°F (20s to 30s°C), a span of up to 20°F (11°C). Rarely, if ever, will temperatures drop below the mid-60s°F (around 15°C) or rise above the mid-90s (about 35°C). (In contrast, it is not uncommon in desert regions for temperatures to vary 50°F or more [38°C] during a 24-hour period.) Now you know why it is often said that "nighttime is the 'winter' of the tropics." This condition also results from atmospheric moisture, which, often in the form of clouds, blocks, absorbs, and reflects back into space some of the incoming solar energy. This prevents temperatures from soaring much higher. At night, atmospheric moisture forms a "blanket" that prevents heat from radiating (escaping) into space, thereby keeping temperatures warmer.

A third anomaly is that your body is a rather poor thermometer—it can be miserable or quite comfortable with the same temperature. Have you ever heard of *sensible temperature, comfort index,* or *heat index*? These terms refer to the same thing: what your body actually senses, or feels, in regard to temperature. The author has lived in both Arizona and several states in the southeastern United States. Ninety degrees in Arizona, with low humidity and a breeze, is very comfortable. The same temperature in the South (or the Wet Tropics), with high humidity and little or no breeze, can be absolutely miserable. How is this difference explained? In scientific terms, it results from the "latent heat of evaporation." This principle can be illustrated as follows: Put some moisture on the back of your hand and then blow on it. Does it feel cool? This is what happens in an arid climate. Humidity is low, and the air can hold much more moisture. Energy is required to convert liquid (perspiration) into vapor (evaporation). Heat energy is thereby lost in the process. Your body is cooled by the evaporation of perspiration into the dry atmosphere. When the

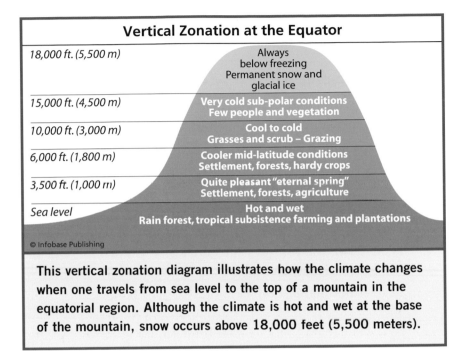

Vertical Zonation at the Equator

18,000 ft. (5,500 m)	**Always below freezing Permanent snow and glacial ice**
15,000 ft. (4,500 m)	**Very cold sub-polar conditions Few people and vegetation**
10,000 ft. (3,000 m)	**Cool to cold Grasses and scrub – Grazing**
6,000 ft. (1,800 m)	**Cooler mid-latitude conditions Settlement, forests, hardy crops**
3,500 ft. (1,000 m)	**Quite pleasant "eternal spring" Settlement, forests, agriculture**
Sea level	**Hot and wet Rain forest, tropical subsistence farming and plantations**

© Infobase Publishing

This vertical zonation diagram illustrates how the climate changes when one travels from sea level to the top of a mountain in the equatorial region. Although the climate is hot and wet at the base of the mountain, snow occurs above 18,000 feet (5,500 meters).

air is saturated (high humidity), as it almost always is in the Wet Tropics, it cannot hold much more moisture. Therefore, perspiration remains on your body, little heat is lost through evaporation, and you remain hot and sticky.

Finally, would you consider taking a *summer* vacation in the tropics? Most people think of the tropics only as a place to escape winter's chill. Surprisingly, the tropics are becoming a popular summer tourist destination as well. Tropical islands of the Caribbean and uplands of Central America, for example, are cooler and more pleasant during the summer months than is about half of the United States. Temperatures drop about 3.5°F with each 1,000-foot increase in elevation (10°C per 1,000 meters). Tropical highlands, therefore, can be "lands of eternal spring," or, at higher elevations, very cold. Higher peaks in Wet Tropical regions do remain snow- (or even glacial-ice) capped throughout the year. Because they are cooler, healthier, and more pleasant, many highland regions support quite high population densities. Europeans, in particular, have been attracted to the more comfortable uplands, such as Central America and the highlands of East Africa.

ATMOSPHERIC PRESSURE AND WINDS

A broad belt of low atmospheric pressure shifts seasonally in a band extending roughly 20 degrees north and south of the equator. Just as water flows from higher to lower elevations, winds blow from regions of high pressure to areas of low pressure. The closer the systems are to one another, and the greater the gradient (the differences in pressure), the greater the wind velocity. Two of Earth's most constant and extreme pressure systems are the low-pressure equatorial "doldrums" and the belt of "horse latitude" high pressure roughly centered over 30 degrees north and south latitude.

The Myth of Weather Extremes

We are fascinated by record-breaking conditions and events. In fact, since it first appeared in 1955, the *Guinness Book of World Records* has sold more copies than any other copyrighted publication. Are the weather extremes that appear in this popular book, official government weather data sources, in textbooks, and in many other sources really correct, though? The answer is, "It depends."

Official weather records are taken by official weather stations that must conform to very rigid conditions. Quite frequently, the author has lived in locations where the daily media's reporting of the state's high or low temperature was higher or lower than that reported for the nation. How can this happen? Several decades ago in the United States, hundreds of then-official weather stations were decommissioned in an attempt to save money. That is, their data were no longer officially recorded

Air is moving almost constantly from the horse latitude high-pressure cells into the equatorial region. In the Northern Hemisphere, the winds blow from the northeast, hence, they are called the northeast trade winds. (Winds take the name of the direction *from* which they blow.) In the Southern Hemisphere, they blow from the southeast, thus, they are called southeast trade winds. Because the conditions that create them are constant, the trade winds are the most reliable of Earth's wind systems. They blow almost constantly and from the same direction. It was this reliability that earned them their name. In the era of sailing vessels, early European navigators sailed southward until reaching about 30 degrees north latitude. There, they found strong winds blowing from the northeast in a southwesterly direction toward America. Because of their

by NOAA (National Oceanic and Atmospheric Administration), even though the "official" equipment continued to record and be monitored on a regular basis. Another problem, of course, is that we have no assurance that extreme conditions actually (and conveniently) occurred at the site where official stations are located. Many areas, such as the vast Amazon and Congo basins, have very few recording stations.

Many times over the years, the author has been asked questions such as, "Why did my thermometer show 140°F (60°C) and the official temperature was only 96°F (35°C)?" Official temperatures are taken above the ground, over a neutral colored surface, and in a shaded box. If you are working outdoors in a nonshaded location, your body is exposed to temperatures much higher—often tens of degrees higher—than those taken under "official" conditions.

velocity and reliability, they soon came to be called the "trade winds," because they facilitated transatlantic trading.

PRECIPITATION

Imagine enough rain falling in one year to reach the top of your head when standing, or even the rooftop of a two-story building! Most of the Wet Tropics receive more than 60 inches (152 centimeters), or 5 feet (1.5 meters), of rainfall each year. Some places receive more than 300 inches (762 centimeters). Year in and year out, Mount Waialeale, located on the Hawaiian island of Kaua'i, lays claim to the title of "the world's wettest spot." It receives a drenching annual average of about 470 inches (1,200 centimeters) of moisture—more than 39 feet (12 meters) of rain. Several locations bordering the Pacific coast of Colombia claim to receive even more moisture. One village claims to receive a whopping (although unofficial) 523 inches (1,328 centimeters) a year! In most Wet Tropical locations, rain falls daily. A "drought" in the rainy tropics is a stretch of several days with just light showers.

A detailed precipitation map will clearly show that there is a sharp divide between places receiving 60 to 100 inches (150 to 250 centimeters) and those receiving much more. This pattern is easily explained by the two dominant controls of precipitation at work in equatorial latitudes, but first you must understand how water vapor (a gas) is converted into liquid (in the tropics, rain). In order to convert water vapor into falling liquid (precipitation), the air must be cooled. This principle can be illustrated by coasters used to protect a table from moisture. When drinking from a glass, can, or bottle containing a cold beverage, moisture can condense (form) on the outside surface of the cold vessel and drip down, creating a ring on the table. So, how does this work in nature?

Rising air cools, and as it cools it can eventually reach what is called the *dew point*—the temperature at which condensation (fog or cloud formation) occurs. This happens because there is a specific minimum amount of moisture that the

Mount Waialeale is the second-highest point (5,208 feet, 1,587 meters) on the Hawaiian island of Kaua'i and is considered the wettest spot on Earth. The mountain averages 470 inches (1,200 centimeters) of rain annually and in 1982 recorded an amazing 683 inches (1,735 centimeters) of precipitation.

atmosphere can hold at any given temperature. Rain, of course, does not fall from all clouds, but with additional cooling, clouds become heavily saturated with moisture, which is then "squeezed" out to fall as precipitation.

Nature cools the atmosphere in several ways. In the Wet Tropics, air is forced aloft to cool and precipitate either *convectionally* or *orographically* (affected by mountains). Convection can be understood by the following simple experiment: Take a lighted match and place your hand a short distance below the flame. Do you feel heat? Now, put your hand palm down well above the flame and begin lowering it. How far is your hand above the flame before you begin to feel heat? Heated air rises. (This principle keeps a hot air balloon aloft.) This is convection, the process of warm air rising. In some locations, moisture-bearing air is also forced aloft orographically. This occurs when winds carry moist air up and over a mountain barrier. Throughout most of the tropics, where the land is relatively flat, all precipitation falls as a result of convectional heating. Where mountains exist, however, the combined convectional and orographic controls contribute to much greater amounts of precipitation. Hawaii's Mount Waialeale, for example, rises abruptly as a 5,208-foot (1,587-meter) barrier lying in the path of the prevailing northeast trade winds. As the moisture-laden winds are forced over the mountain, they cool, their moisture condenses, and rain pours from the clouds almost daily.

This orographic effect gives rise to one of nature's most unexpected contrasts. Within just a few miles of Mount Waialeale, downwind from the peak in the mountain's *rain shadow* (dry leeward side), precipitation drops by about 95 percent to only about 25 inches (60 centimeters). As the wind descends down the leeward side (the downwind side) of the mountain, the air warms, thereby increasing its moisture-holding capacity. Rather than raining, moisture is evaporated from the surface, creating an almost desert-like landscape. Brazil's eastern tip lies in the rain shadow of the Brazilian Highlands. It is an area of semiaridity, resulting in chronic poverty for its primarily agricultural people.

STORMS

Storms can be defined as extreme conditions of wind and/ or precipitation. Surprisingly, perhaps, the Wet Tropics are relatively storm free. It may seem strange, but the more precipitation an area receives, the less damage it experiences from flooding. This is because both nature and human activities are well adapted to receiving large amounts of moisture. Ample vegetation slows runoff, and a well-developed drainage network of streams exists. Humans also know where flooding can

Hurricanes commonly occur in the tropics and can inflict serious damage due to strong winds, heavy rain, and coastal storm surge. Pictured here are boats that have been piled together in the harbor of St. George's, Grenada, after Hurricane Ivan swept through the region in September 2004.

be expected and can avoid settling in or developing such areas. Simply stated, both nature and humans are prepared.

Only one type of severe storm occurs with some regularity in the tropical latitudes: tropical cyclones. Although the storms are fundamentally the same, they go by several names: hurricanes (in the Atlantic and eastern Pacific Basin), typhoons (in the central and western Pacific), and cyclones (in the northeastern Indian Ocean). During recent years, residents of the United States have learned a great deal about these intense low-pressure systems and their accompanying howling winds. They have killed several thousand people, inflicted billions of dollars of damage, and done incalculable harm to the environment.

The storms begin as low-pressure systems, usually at the poleward edge of the Wet Tropics. (Most form between 7 and 15 degrees north latitude, although they occasionally occur in the Southern Hemisphere.) In the Northern Hemisphere, they drift westward to northwestward, usually gaining intensity as they continue to cross warm, tropical waters, on which they "feed." Because of their movement, they affect the eastern side of continental areas, with western margins being relatively free of their fury. Winds can reach 200 miles (320 kilometers) per hour. Severe flooding is often caused by drenching rains, often exceeding 40 inches (100 centimeters) during a storm's passing. In addition, along coasts, wind-lashed waves can reach 20 feet (6 meters) or more in height and destroy everything in their path as they surge inland. Crops such as sugarcane, coconut and other palms, bananas, and cacao are destroyed by high winds and may take years to recover. The human toll, in terms of loss and suffering, can be immeasurable.

LIVING IN THE WET TROPICS

People adjust to conditions of weather and climate regardless of where they live. The Inuit understand Arctic living just as Bedouin nomads are at home in the Sahara Desert. Although the Wet Tropics may seem "harsh" to most midlatitude peoples, the opposite actually is true. Warm temperatures, constant moisture, resulting dense plant growth, and reliable winds are not going to jeopardize life. Of all the world's climates, in fact, the Wet Tropics are in many ways the least challenging. Drenching rains, parching drought, early-autumn or late-spring crop-killing frost, and stifling hot or frigidly cold spells are commonplace throughout much of the world. So are damaging winds, devastating hail storms, and other examples of nature's atmospheric fury unleashed. With the exception of tropical cyclones in some areas, none of these conditions occur in the Wet Tropics. Temperatures rarely fluctuate more than a few degrees. Frost, hail, tornadoes, and drought do not occur. Precipitation rarely varies by more than about 10 percent from year to year. When "extreme environment" is used in reference to the Wet Tropics (extremes of temperature and moisture), it does not necessarily mean that these lands are poorly suited for human life.

Humans throughout the Wet Tropics schedule their daily activities in such a way that they are well adapted to temperature conditions. Many activities take place early in the morning, often before sunrise. By late morning, most activity ceases. The author once rode a bicycle across Cayenne, French Guiana's capital city (in South America), around noon and did not see a single person on the street or commercial establishment open. During the heat of the day, people dine, nap, socialize, or engage in other activities that are less affected by the intense heat and humidity. By late afternoon, when temperatures begin cooling, however, activity resumes and continues on well into the evening.

Temperature and precipitation are perhaps the key elements that influence other aspects of the natural environment. In the following chapter, you will learn how climate has helped fashion other natural features of the Wet Tropics.

3

Land and Water Features

In the previous chapter, you learned how the atmosphere and its conditions affect, indeed define, the Wet Tropics. This chapter focuses upon the region's land, soil, and water features.

LAND FEATURES

Unlike the other Extreme Environments included in this series— polar and desert lands—there really are no major landform features that are unique to the Wet Tropics. The process of rock weathering (decomposition and disintegration of rock material) proceeds at a rapid rate, leaving many surfaces rock free. Because of the high amounts of precipitation, moving water is the primary agent of erosion. Some locations have spectacular erosional terrain, and throughout the Wet Tropics, river valleys, basins, and coastal plains have deep layers of often rich alluvium (water-deposited sediments).

Of Earth's major land features—plains, plateaus, hills, and mountains—all occur within the region. South America's Amazon Basin is one of the world's greatest plains and home to its most mighty river. Hills and mountains, including the lofty Andes, also lie within the continent's Wet Tropics. In Ecuador, volcanic Mount Chimborazo rises to a snow- and glacier-clad 20,702 feet (6,310 meters), within miles of the equator. The rugged Guiana Highlands, located in northeastern South America, between the Orinoco and Amazon rivers, is one of the world's most remote regions. Here, strange-looking, flat-topped mountains called tepuis rise abruptly from the surrounding plains. This is the area that inspired such classic books (and later motion pictures) as W. H. Hudson's *Green Mansions* and Arthur Conan Doyle's *The Lost World*.

Much of Africa, including the Wet Tropical portion, is a plateau surface, bordered by a very narrow coastal plain. In eastern equatorial Africa, high volcanic peaks rise above surrounding plains, plateaus, and Africa's huge scar, the Great Rift Valley. The highest peak, majestic snowcapped Mount Kilimanjaro, reaches an elevation of 19,340 feet (5,895 meters). Increasing global temperatures of recent decades, however, are rapidly melting the snow and small glaciers that have given the volcano its spectacular sparkling white crown.

The islands and peninsulas of Southeast Asia offer a combination of mountains and plains. Here, some volcanic peaks rise above 14,000 feet (4,270 meters). Elsewhere, tropical islands lie scattered across portions of the Indian, Atlantic, and Pacific oceans. Many owe their origin to volcanic activity. Some are formed from coral reefs that grew to create a semicircular atoll around a volcano (many of which are now submerged). These low-lying, nearly flat, islands have little water and poor soil. Few of them support large populations. Generally speaking, the mountainous islands are more densely populated. They have better soil, more water (because of increased orographic precipitation), and a more varied environment for agriculture.

In 1883, Indonesia suffered yet another violent volcanic eruption, this time Mount Krakatoa. The explosion sent an estimated six cubic miles (25 cubic kilometers) of debris into the atmosphere and created the loudest sound ever heard by humans. In fact, the explosive roar was heard as far away as islands in the western Indian Ocean, a distance of several thousand miles. An estimated 35,000 to 40,000 people lost their lives in the area immediately surrounding the island, and tens of thousands more were swept away by the resulting tsunami.

The Caribbean region, too, has suffered a volcanic catastrophe. In 1902, Mount Pelée, on the small island of Martinique, erupted violently. In what was to be the worst volcanic disaster of the twentieth century, about 26,000 people lost their lives as the eruption destroyed the city of Saint-Pierre.

TROPICAL SOILS

Until the early twentieth century, it was widely believed that tropical soils were the world's most fertile and those of desert lands the least fertile. After all, as anyone could see, tropical soils support the world's most diverse ecosystem, the tropical rain forest, and deserts are all but void of vegetation. Gradually, however, pedologists (scientists who study soils) began to realize that just the opposite is true: Most tropical soils are among the very least fertile (and where they exist, desert soils are among the most fertile).

Two primary factors explain the lack of fertility associated with most tropical soils. First, because of the heavy amounts of precipitation they receive, the soils are heavily leached. Leaching is the process by which moisture takes minerals (think of them as the soil's "vitamins" and other nutrients) into solution and removes them from the soil. Much of the fertility contained in soils comes from decayed organic matter—decayed roots, leaves, and even woody portions of plants. In the tropics, however, organic decay is so rapid that little humus (the organic upper layer of soil) is formed. As long as the soils are supporting a growth of lush tropical rain forest, some fertility is maintained. Organic matter from the overlying forest is returned to the soil as a part of the normal life cycle. When the forest is removed, however, the cycle is broken, and the soil very rapidly becomes infertile. This is why most tropical subsistence agricultural plots (as you will learn later) must shift location every few years. It also explains why cutting the rain forests in the hope of expanding commercial farmland—as is occurring in Brazil's Amazon rain forest—is a very unwise environmental practice.

Not all tropical soils are infertile; there are two major exceptions. After all, some tropical areas are home to huge tropical plantations that produce specialty crops for midlatitude markets. The answer lies in what is called the "parent material" from which the soil is formed. Some tropical locations have soils formed from rich volcanic ash. Such conditions are found in some valleys in Central America, the Central Andes, East Africa, and Indonesia. A second condition is where streams deposit fertile alluvium (silt) in their floodplain (the valley through which they flow) or near their delta. Many coastal plains, for example, have rich alluvial soils that support a booming plantation economy. It was the fertile coastal plain of tropical Brazil that first attracted Portuguese sugar growers to South America.

Anyone traveling in the Wet Tropics (or, for that matter, the southeastern United States) is sure to notice the deep red color of most soils. Silica (silt) and components of iron and aluminum are usually major elements. In the tropics, much of the silica is leached from the soil, leaving oxides of iron and aluminum. It is the iron oxide (literally, rust) that gives tropical soils their characteristic red color. And if you look at a map of bauxite (the ore from which aluminum is manufactured), you will notice that much of it comes from the tropics. That is because tropical soils also are rich in aluminum oxide.

WATER FEATURES

For much of the world, water has become a scarce and precious resource. This certainly is not true within the Wet Tropics! In fact, the region is home to the world's two largest rivers, the Amazon and Congo, the biggest waterfalls, and some very unique lakes. Only the Polar regions have more freshwater— and there, much of it is locked up in the form of ice and is of little use.

Rivers

Rivers, as one would expect in a region receiving large amounts of rainfall, are numerous and huge in the Wet Tropics. In fact, the Amazon alone carries about one-fifth of the entire world's river water—just one of the many "Wow!" features of this giant stream (see sidebar on page 38). The river resembles a huge tree, with roots at the mouth and its branches reaching into uplands scattered in all directions. Literally thousands of streams, draining an area nearly the size of the 48 contiguous U.S. states, contribute to the Amazon's gigantic flow. Some of the tributaries, such as the Rio Negro, themselves rank among the world's largest rivers.

The Amazon flows roughly parallel to and just a few degrees south of the equator. Its main channel, as well as most upper tributaries, flow from the high Andes. As the streams plunge down the eastern slopes of the mountains, they gnaw away huge amounts of earth. This silt makes the main stream of the river yellow in color. Streams flowing in from the north, such as the Rio Negro (Black River), flow over very flat, low-lying land, and hence, flow very slowly. Their water is the color of coffee or tea for the same reason—the water contains leaves and other organic matter. Most streams entering the Amazon from the south flow across rocky terrain, resulting in their water being quite clear. On both the north and south, the Wet Tropics is bordered by regions of wet and dry tropical climate (with rain falling during the summer, or high sun season). Therefore, the Amazon maintains a fairly constant level. During roughly six months of the year, streams flowing from the north are in flood stage, followed by a half year of floodwater flowing from the south.

This aerial view of the Amazon River illustrates the grandeur of the world's largest river (in terms of water volume). Pictured here is the city of Manaus, Brazil, which lies near the confluence of the Amazon and the Negro rivers.

The Congo River flows westward across equatorial Africa. In both size of drainage basin and volume of stream flow, the Congo trails only the mighty Amazon among the world's great rivers. Unlike the Amazon, which is navigable to ocean-going vessels for more than 2,000 miles (3,200 kilometers), the Congo plunges over navigation-limiting cataracts within about 100 miles (160 kilometers) from its mouth in the Atlantic Ocean. Just above the rapids that form Livingstone Falls, the river widens to form Malebo Pool (formerly Stanley Pool). This large lake-like feature is more than 20 miles (32 kilometers) long and about 14 miles (23 kilometers) wide. Two capital cities, Brazzaville (Congo) and Kinshasa (Democratic Republic of the Congo), face one another across the lower

The Amazon River
One of the Wonders of the Natural World

Here are several facts about this amazing South American river:
- It is the world's largest river in terms of volume, containing about 20 percent of all river flow.
- It is 4,000 miles (6,437 kilometers) long, ranking second in length, behind the Nile (about 100 miles [161 kilometers] shorter).
- Its drainage basin occupies some 2.7 million square miles (6.9 million square kilometers), or nearly 40 percent of the South American continent.
- Its volume is four times greater than the Congo River, which has the second-greatest flow.
- Its volume is about 17 times greater than that of the Mississippi River.
- Its source is Lake Lauricocha, in the Peruvian Andes, about 100 miles (161 kilometers) from the Pacific Ocean.
- It has 1,100 major tributaries, with a combined length of about 4 million miles (6.43 million kilometers).
- Seven of its tributaries are more than 1,000 miles (1,610 kilometers) long.

end of the pool. Because the Congo flows across a somewhat rugged plateau surface, it has many falls and rapids that limit its use for navigation. These conditions do, however, offer tremendous potential for hydroelectric development.

Many tropical islands, including those of Southeast Asia, have small streams of local importance. Elsewhere, many rivers associated with other climates and regions actually have their headwaters in the Wet Tropics. South America's Orinoco River flows from the western part of the Amazon Basin eastward across Venezuela's *llanos* (savanna grasslands). In Africa, both

- It is navigable to oceangoing vessels to Iquitos, Peru (2,300 miles, or 3,700 kilometers).
- It varies in width from 1 to 35 miles (1.6 to 56 kilometers), and in many places land cannot be seen across the river.
- Each day, as much water is discharged from the Amazon as New York City uses in nine years.
- Its discharge creates a surface lens of freshwater that reaches up to 200 miles (320 kilometers) into the Atlantic.
- It is 150 to 200 miles (240 to 320 kilometers) wide at its mouth.
- Its channel in Brazil has an average depth of 150 feet (46 meters), reaching 400 feet (122 meters) in places.
- It transports up to 3 million tons of sediment each day.
- A tidal bore (an upstream surge of water resulting from the rising Atlantic tide) creates a "wall" of water up to 15 feet (4.6 meters) high, which travels upstream at 30 miles per hour (48 kilometers per hour) at the river's mouth.

the Niger and the Nile begin in Wet Tropical highlands. The Nile is the world's most important exotic river—a stream that flows throughout the year through a desert landscape, creating an oasis.

Throughout much of the Amazon and Congo basins, surface travel is limited to streams. With few exceptions, rivers are the highways of the tropics. Highway building, in fact, is difficult if not impossible throughout much of the tropical realm because of the rivers. They are so numerous and so wide that bridging the many streams is cost prohibitive. Not a single bridge crosses the Amazon or any of its major tributaries, and only one, located near its mouth and the city of Matadi, spans the Congo River. Where warranted by population and traffic flow, ferries provide service. Rivers are also a chief source of food for most people living along their shores.

To date, there has been very little development of the region's hydroelectric potential. The Amazon flows across flat terrain and is far too wide to dam. In addition, the basin supports a very small population and line loss limits the distance that power can be transmitted. The Congo River ranks among the world's leading streams in hydroelectric potential. But the region lacks the population and capital resources to justify the expenditure of harnessing the stream.

Lakes

Approximately 90 percent of all the world's natural lakes were formed by glacial action. For this reason, and despite the huge amounts of surface moisture available, very few lakes dot the Wet Tropical landscape. Several large freshwater bodies lie near the edge of the region. In South America, Lake Titicaca lies tucked away in the Central Andes at an elevation of 12,536 feet (3,821 meters), making it the highest commercially navigable lake in the world. It is also the largest freshwater lake in South America. There are two large lakes in the Central American country of Nicaragua: Lake Nicaragua and the smaller Lake Managua. In Panama, Lake Gatún plays a very important role

Located on the border of Peru and Bolivia, Lake Titicaca is the world's highest commercially navigable lake at an elevation of 12,536 feet (3,821 meters). Pictured here is an Ayamara man working among the terraces where his people grow crops such as potatoes.

in the Panama Canal. Its freshwater serves as a filter that prevents saltwater species from passing between the Atlantic and Pacific, thereby possibly upsetting the ecological balance of the oceans' tropical waters.

Africa's Lake Victoria has a surface area of 26,564 square miles (68,800 square kilometers), making it the world's second-largest freshwater lake, surpassed in area only by North America's Lake Superior. The main channel of the Nile River begins where the Rippon Falls once cascaded from the lake. (The falls were submerged by the reservoir that formed behind a dam built in the 1950s.) A short distance southwest of Lake

Victoria, occupying a depression in eastern Africa's Great Rift Valley, is Lake Tanganyika. This long, narrow, "stringbean"-shaped water body reaches a depth of 4,820 feet (1,470 meters). Only Siberia's Lake Baikal is deeper.

Two other lakes warrant special mention—Africa's Lake Monoun and Lake Nyos, both of which are in Cameroon. In the mid-1980s, both water bodies "erupted" clouds of deadly carbon dioxide that killed nearly 1,800 people. Scientists believe that the sudden release of lethal gas could occur again in these and possibly other lakes within the region.

Waterfalls

The Guiana Highlands are one of Earth's most remote and inaccessible places, which helps explain why the world's highest waterfall was not discovered until 1935! In that year, American pilot Jimmy Angel spotted the spectacular cataract that bears his name through a break in the clouds that almost constantly blanket the region. From near the crest of a flat-topped *tepui*, Angel Falls plummets 2,648 feet (807 meters) in a single drop, followed by a second fall of 564 feet (172 meters)—a total drop of 3,212 feet (979 meters)!

Availability of water resources is of little concern to most of the Wet Tropics. Water pollution, however, is a growing problem in many locations. The Amazon River, despite the few people living in its basin, is beginning to suffer the effects of choking silt. Mercury and other deadly toxins seep into its waters from mining operations in the area. In Africa, lakes Victoria and Tanganyika are beginning to suffer the ill effects of polluting runoff that enters from inflowing rivers and sewage from bordering villages.

Weather and climate, land features, and water features form important parts of a region's ecosystem—all those natural elements that form an interrelated system of organisms and the environment in which they live. In the following chapter, you will visit the vast and dense tropical rain forest and its abundant wildlife.

4

Tropical Rain Forest Ecosystems

The dense forest reaches skyward, its thick overhead canopy casting an eerie green shadow on the soggy floor below. You are surrounded by an almost claustrophobic wall of thick vegetation that seems to be closing in on every side. Each tree is festooned with thousands of smaller plants that cling to the towering giants for support. Vines resembling huge serpents tightly hug each tree as they climb upward in search of life-giving sunlight. Roots of many arboreal plants hang from high above, like long tentacles. Not a leaf stirs in the dead-still atmosphere. Drenching humidity makes the sultry air feel much like a steam bath, and every breath is permeated by the strong odor of decaying vegetation.

Sounds of the rain forest seem to present a never-ending concert. There is the constant low hum of mosquitoes and other insects swarming about in a dizzying cloud. High above, birds provide a crescendo of chirps, squawks, songs, and whistles. Occasionally, the blood-curdling roar, howl, or cry of some distant and perhaps unknown animal sends shivers up one's spine. Could a deadly venomous snake be lurking beneath those leaves or that log, or on that branch just above your head? Might a huge boa constrictor or crocodile, or a deadly piranha, be lurking just beneath the mantle of huge lily pads covering the river's surface? You are about to enter the world's most diverse ecosystem and one of its most expansive. Welcome to the tropical rain forest!

CHARACTERISTICS OF THE TROPICAL RAIN FOREST

Vegetation thrives under conditions of constantly high temperatures and ample moisture. The rain forests of tropical South America and Africa are the world's third- and fourth-largest forested regions, respectively. In area, they are surpassed only by the vast taiga forests that stretch across northern North America and Eurasia. The Wet Tropical environment is so favorable to life that an estimated 80 percent of the world's plant and animal species are native to the region. Christopher Columbus provided the first known description of the tropical rain forest by a European. Upon his arrival on the Caribbean island of Hispañola, he wrote:

> The island is filled with trees of a thousand kinds and tall, and they seem to touch the sky. And I am told that they never lose their foliage, as I can understand, for I saw them as green and as lovely as they are in Spain in May and some of them were flowering, some bearing fruit, and some in another stage, according to their nature.

Dominant characteristics of the tropical rain forest (also called "selva," derived from the Spanish *La Selva*) include the following features and conditions:

- **Most trees are broadleaf (rather than needleleaf) evergreens**. They have broad leaves that are lost continuously, rather than seasonally. In the Wet Tropics, there are no

Many species of plants and trees coexist within a small area in the tropical rain forest. Tropical rain forests, such as this one in Africa, can support up to 2,500 species of trees.

seasonal changes to trigger a period of plant dormancy. At any time of the year, a single tree may be experiencing all stages of the normal midlatitude annual growth cycle.

- **A vast number of species exist within a small area**. Four hundred or more tree species may occupy a single square

mile area. Southeast Asia supports some 3,000 species
of trees. The African and American tropics are not far
behind, with some 2,500 species each.

- **Forests are three-tiered**. When mature, rain forest trees
  form three tiers or layers of forest vegetation. The tallest
  trees grow to heights of 150 to 200 feet (45 to 60 meters).
  A second tier grows to an average of 80 to 120 feet (25
  to 35 meters). Finally, a lower group of trees mature at
  heights reaching only 40 to 60 feet (10 to 20 meters).

- **A dense overhead canopy blocks sunlight**. The "eerie
  green shadow" referred to in the opening paragraph of
  this chapter is the result of a dense overhead canopy
  formed by the crowns of trees. Despite the bright tropical
  sunlight, the forest floor is so dark that it is very difficult
  to take photographs within the rain forest. In the absence
  of direct sunlight (hence, photosynthesis), there is little
  plant life on the forest floor.

- **Some species have unique lower trunks**. Flaring buttresses are common among many tree species. Buttresses
  may extend as high as 25 feet (7.5 meters) and flare out
  10 to 20 feet (3 to 6 meters) from the base. Coastal man-
  groves have several dozen stilt-like roots that rise above
  the water supporting each tree. Their complex root system catches silt, thereby stabilizing shorelines and often
  creating islands or shoals in streams.

- **Many trees have long, straight trunks and few lower
  branches**. The trunks of most species have few, if any,
  limbs before the broad crowns that spread much like an
  umbrella to capture life-giving sunlight.

- **Each tree is host to a vast array of other plants**. Tens
  of thousands of vines, creepers, mosses, ferns, and other
  plants cling to their tree hosts. Some are epiphytic; that
  is, they attach themselves to the host for support, but do
  not gain nourishment from the tree. Some such plants,
  including various species of bromeliads, are quite large.
  Several varieties of orchids are also epiphytic. Roots of

epiphytes are a common sight as they descend in clusters, dangling in midair to draw moisture and nourishment from the air. Many other plants are parasites; they both cling to and gain their nourishment from their host.

- **Trees support many lianas (vines).** Many, if not most, trees in the rain forest serve as host to lianas, large vines that can be as thick as a human's arm or even thigh. The vines grow upward in search of sunlight. Upon reaching the canopy, they also grow outward, and may reach lengths of many hundreds of feet. Lianas often become so enmeshed in the crowns that if trees are cut, they will not fall because the lianas hold them up!

- **Vegetation changes with elevation.** Tropical rain forest is seldom found above 3,500 feet (1,070 meters). In mountainous regions, depending on local conditions of temperature and humidity (the dew point), there is often a zone that experiences almost constant fog. Here, an "elfin" or cloud forest develops. Ferns, mosses, and other moisture-living plants thrive, giving the landscape a fairyland-like appearance.

Forest Rain in the Rain Forest

Imagine awakening, crawling out of your "jungle hammock," and suddenly being drenched with rain falling from a cloudless sky! This seemingly incongruous event happens frequently in the tropical rain forest. Early morning, just at sunrise, is usually the coldest time of the day. Trees, of course, lose moisture through *transpiration*, the passing off of water vapor. This vapor, in turn, condenses to form dew on the leaves high overhead in the canopy-forming crowns of the forest trees. With the slightest breeze, the leaves begin to flutter and the accumulated dew falls to the forest floor as "rain."

The tropical rain forest is also widely misunderstood. Not only is it subject to many myths, but it is also a very fragile ecosystem that is disappearing at an alarming rate in some locations. The remainder of this chapter focuses on these themes and the abundant animal life that thrives in the rain forest habitat.

MYTHS AND MISCONCEPTIONS

As you already have learned, a number of false beliefs are held regarding Wet Tropical temperatures and soil fertility. The same is true for the world's rain forests—perhaps the world's most mysterious, least understood, and myth-tainted ecosystem.

No myth is more widespread than the almost universal notion (at least in the United States and Canada) that *jungle* and *tropical rain forest* are one and the same. This myth appears to have been promoted by the Edgar Rice Burroughs series of *Tarzan* books. Burroughs used the term *jungle* in the place of *rain forest*—a densely wooded environment, with dangling vines on which Tarzan could easily swing from tree to tree. In reality, the rain forest's thick overhead canopy blocks sunlight from reaching the ground level. In the absence of sunlight (hence, little photosynthesis), very little plant life grows, leaving the forest floor quite open. Jungle, on the other hand, refers to a very dense and almost impenetrable growth of vegetation. It occurs only where sunlight reaches the forest floor. Such conditions occur in and along the edge of clearings such as roads, railroads, rivers, villages, or agricultural fields. These environments, of course, are the kinds of places most visitors to the tropics see during their travels. As a result, the myth that all rain forest is jungle continues to be widely held.

The nature of plant life is also widely misunderstood. Many people think of the rain forest as an environment featuring mainly herbaceous (nonwoody) plants. Actually, woody species (trees) dominate the ecosystem. It is also commonly believed that the rain forest is a place ablaze with vividly colored blossoms of flowering plants. In reality, the flowers of most wild plants are quite drab. Shades of dull green, brown, and yellow tend to dominate. One noteworthy exception is the Flamboyant tree, with its spectacular display of flame-colored blossoms. There are, of course, many beautiful flowering tropical plants that have been domesticated and are cultivated.

During recent decades, much has been written about the widespread deforestation occurring within the world's rain forests. This has led many people to believe that the cutting is for commercial purposes relating to the wood (lumber, timber) itself. This is rarely the case. Nearly all deforestation is the result of land clearing for agricultural purposes. Commercial logging is limited to a few relatively small areas, such as in Southeast Asia. Throughout most of the world's rain forests, timber cutting faces numerous handicaps. First, only tropical hardwoods such at teak and mahogany are valuable. These valuable trees are so few in number and so widely scattered that it is difficult if not impossible to locate and harvest them. Additionally, because of their density, hardwoods do not float. In the absence of roadways or railroads, it is extremely difficult and costly to move a harvested tree from the forest. Most trees in the tropical forest are softwoods having little economic value. These reasons help explain why tropical hardwoods command such a high price and are used so sparingly.

AN ENDANGERED ECOSYSTEM

Today, the tropical rain forest is one of Earth's most important, yet endangered, ecosystems. In Latin America, it is estimated that at least 10 percent of the 2-million-square-mile (5.2-million-square-kilometer) Amazon rain forest has been cut during recent decades. One-third of Indonesia's rain forest has been lost during the past 15 years. Worldwide, about 0.6 to 0.7 percent of the world's tropical forest is destroyed each year. Small farmers, practicing traditional slash-burn, shifting cultivation, are responsible for perhaps half of the destruction. The rest is attributed to clearing land for commercial farming, ranching,

Approximately 0.6 to 0.7 percent of tropical rain forests worldwide are destroyed each year. In the Amazon rain forest, ranchers, soybean farmers, and loggers are the primary culprits in setting fires such as this one near the northern Brazilian city of Sao Felix do Xingu.

building transportation routes, mining, lumbering (much of which is illegal), human settlements, or some other purpose. Little, if any, of the original rain forest remains in tropical Africa, and it is disappearing rapidly in Southeast Asia.

Many scientists have expressed great concern over the loss of the world's tropical rain forests. Geographer William Denevan has cited a number of consequences resulting from deforestation in tropical South America. In the Amazon, fully half the atmospheric moisture falling as rain is believed to come from the trees themselves (through evapotranspiration). If the forest is destroyed, drought may follow. When the forest is removed, tropical Oxisols (lateritic soils—red in color, with a high content in the oxides of iron and hydroxide of aluminum) tend to harden, much like the process of brick-making. Such soils, of course, are useless for farming, livestock ranching, or any other purpose. In the absence of an adequate ground cover, rainwater runs off more rapidly, causing erosion and greater fluctuations in stream flow. Wildlife habitat is destroyed, resulting in the extinction or removal of many animal species.

There are many other reasons why we should be deeply concerned over the loss of the world's tropical rain forests. Forests serve as "scrubbers" of atmospheric pollutants, including those that may be causing global warming. As rain forests dwindle in area, perhaps countless species, many as yet unknown or unidentified, may be lost forever. With them may be lost many plants offering medical benefits, such as a cure for cancer or even the common cold. And, of course, many things of economic value are produced by rain forest trees and other plants. As outsiders move into the rain forest, native cultures often suffer or even vanish. The Amazon Basin is the only place in the world where at least some original rain forest cover remains. How long will this treasure house remain? Only time will tell. Protecting the remaining tropical rain forests should be one of the world's primary environmental concerns.

ANIMAL LIFE OF THE WET TROPICS

"Scientists Search for Ancient Dinosaurs in Africa's Congo Region". . ."Lost World of Untouched Species Found in New Guinea". . ."Scientists to Hunt 'Bigfoot' in Malaysian Rain forest". . ."New Tribe Discovered in Remote Area of Amazon." These story lines are typical of dozens collected by the author during recent years. They reveal a fundamental truth about this fascinating region: Much of the world's rain forest remains relatively unknown to scientists and other outsiders.

Animal life in the Wet Tropics, like the region's flora, or plant life, is amazingly diverse. Estimates vary, but it is believed that more than 80 percent of all living species inhabit the tropical ecosystem. It is home to some 85 percent of the world's bird species, as well as perhaps one-half million differ-ent varieties of insects. Waters teem with thousands of kinds of fish and other aquatic life—some of which can be deadly. Land animals, too, are numerous and varied.

Large Animals of the Wet Tropics

Surprisingly, perhaps, very few large animals inhabit the rain forest. In South America, the largest is the manatee. This strange-looking creature lives in water, eats only vegetation, can grow to a length of 15 feet (5 meters), and weighs up to one ton. The largest land animal is the tapir. This equally strange-looking herbivore has been described as "a pig that started out as an elephant, decided it wanted to be a horse, then changed its mind again." Both animals are threatened with extinction because of their highly prized flesh. Other large animals of the region include many kinds of rodents (including the large capybara), giant anteaters, jaguars, and ocelots. There are also many kinds of monkeys, including the howler whose cry is the loudest animal sound in nature, sounding much like a jet plane.

In Africa, most large animals inhabit the savanna grass-lands that border the rain forest. Elephants and rhinoceros, for example, thrive within the zone between the savanna and rain forest but rarely are found deep within the forest itself. The seriously endangered gorilla is the largest animal in Wet Tropical Africa. Once common throughout the region, today their numbers have dwindled to fewer than 100,000.

Gorillas are the largest living primates, with males weigh-ing up to 600 pounds (270 kilograms). They and their smaller cousin, the African chimpanzee, also share the distinction of being our closest living relatives. Gorillas and chimpanzees are mainly vegetarian, eating tender shoots, leaves, fruits, and insects for an occasional snack.

The dense forest of the central Congo Basin is home to one of the world's strangest animals, the okapi. About the size of a horse, it has the horns and anatomical structure of a giraffe.

One of the strangest animals that lives in the dense forest of Africa's Congo Basin is the okapi. This unusual mammal has stripes like a zebra but also resembles a giraffe, which is one of its closest relatives.

Its legs resemble those of the zebra in both size and stripes, and its hooves are much like those of oxen. The okapi's body trunk is similar to that of an antelope, and its eyes most closely function like those of a chameleon. Its blue tongue is exceeded in length only by that of the anteater! Tropical Asia's largest animal is the elephant. Most are found in the monsoon tropical region of South Asia, although small populations exist in Southeast Asia.

Throughout the tropical world, many if not most large animals are threatened with extinction. As human populations grow, wildlife habitat becomes increasingly threatened or even destroyed. This is particularly true in much of the African and Asian tropics. Elephant populations have dwindled as poachers have killed thousands of these magnificent animals for their ivory tusks. The same holds true for the black rhino, the horns of which are more valuable than gold to some Asian cultures. Perhaps the greatest threat comes from the widespread practice of killing animals for *bush meat*—a catchall term for wildlife meat consumed by humans. In South America, both the manatee and tapir are threatened with extinction because of their prized flesh. In Africa, chimpanzee, gorilla, and elephant meat sell at double the price of beef or pork in many markets. Today, most countries have laws prohibiting poaching and the taking of bush meat, but poor, hungry native peoples often pay little attention to such laws, and enforcement is often lax.

Most Common Fauna of the Wet Tropics

Volumes easily could be written describing tropical insects, birds, fish, and other fauna. Nothing is more apt to impress (or depress, as the case may be) a visitor than the region's innumerable insects. Mosquitoes, flies, and gnats are seemingly everywhere. So, too, are ants, lice, fleas, ticks, beetles, spiders, and countless other flying, creeping, and crawling things. Some are spectacular, like many butterflies, including the beautiful blue iridescent morphos of tropical Latin America. Many insects are little more than a nuisance. A few, however, can be deadly. The bite or sting of venomous spiders and scorpions can kill directly. Most dangerous insects, however, transmit such potentially lethal diseases as malaria, yellow fever, and sleeping sickness. Fortunately, some tropical diseases can now be controlled, and steps are underway in many locations to eradicate them permanently. Others, such as malaria, continue to take a deadly toll. Occasionally, new diseases such as HIV/AIDS or Ebola emerge, often with devastating results.

Birdlife is also extremely varied. Birds' varied sounds create an orchestration of delightful "music" that will long be remembered by visitors to the rain forest. Some species exhibit a spectacular array of colors, making them highly visible as they dart from perch to perch among the trees. Others are grotesque, like the skulking black vultures that seem to constantly lurk in search of a dead morsel upon which to feast.

Tropical waters teem with fish, including hundreds of species that are the chief source of protein for millions of people. Some varieties, such as South America's pirarucú and catfish common throughout most of the area, can be giants. One catfish caught in tropical Southeast Asia in 2005 weighed a whopping 646 pounds (293 kilograms). Any visitor to the tropics absolutely must visit a fish market at the break of dawn. The varied sizes, shapes, colors, and general appearances of the catch are absolutely amazing!

Some freshwater species can be deadly, however. Crocodiles thrive throughout the tropical realm and beyond, and American alligators and the smaller caiman add to the list of fierce giant reptiles. Each region has its own kind(s) of dangerous fish. None is better known or more notorious than South America's deadly piranha. These ravenous carnivores have large, powerful jaws and razor-sharp teeth. They travel in schools and can strip a large animal to bare bones in a matter of minutes.

Things You Want to See Only in a Zoo

You may want to see some forms of tropical life only in a zoo. The rain forest teems with potentially dangerous species. Southeast Asia, alone, is home to some 450 to 500 varieties of snakes, many of which are highly venomous. These include the deadly coral snake, banded krait, king cobra, and several

The Komodo dragon is the largest lizard in the world; it can grow up to 10 feet (3 meters) in length and weigh more than 200 pounds (90 kilograms). Native to Indonesia, Komodos often live up to 30 years in the wild.

kinds of vipers. The African and American tropics also have hundreds of reptiles. South America's huge bushmaster is the world's largest venomous snake. The giant killer can grow to 25 feet (7.5 meters) in length. Size alone, however, is not a valid measure of how deadly a snake can be. Many varieties scarcely a foot (0.3 meters) in length can inflict a fatal bite.

"Which snake is the world's largest?" is a question subject to considerable debate. South America's anaconda, a water boa constrictor, can grow to 30 feet (10 meters) and weigh up to 550 pounds (250 kilograms). Unofficial accounts, however, have these monsters growing to twice that length. For some time, the largest "official" record was held by a Burmese python that measured 32 feet (9.75 meters) and weighed just over 400 pounds (183 kilograms). This record was smashed in 2003 by an Indonesian reticulated python captured on the island of Java. According to officials, the giant measured an unbelievable 49 feet (15 meters) in length, was 2.8 feet (0.85 meters) in diameter, and weighed 992 pounds (450 kilograms)!

Indonesia also is home to the Komodo dragon, the world's largest and most dangerous lizard. An estimated 2,500 to 5,000 of these huge reptiles are found on a small number of islands, including Flores and Komodo. They can reach 10 feet (3 meters) in length and weigh more than 200 pounds (90 kilograms). These giants can run as fast as humans over a short distance and are excellent swimmers. Although the dragons have excellent eyesight and sharp claws, it is their bite that kills. The Komodo's mouth contains deadly bacteria that, when the Komodo bites, causes infections from which their prey eventually dies.

Just How Dangerous Are the Tropics?

Many, if not most, environments and ecosystems hold potential dangers to human life. Are the Wet Tropics more dangerous than other regions? Not necessarily. As is true when traveling in any location, visitors must use common sense and exercise caution. Much of what we "know" about dangers lurking in the tropics comes from Hollywood's portrayal of the region. (The 1997 film *Anaconda* immediately comes to mind.)

The author of this book once spent nearly three months conducting research in "The Bush" of tropical South America. He swam daily in the rivers, traveled the streams by dugout canoe, walked through miles of rain forest, and slept nightly in a hammock. During the period, he saw only one small, non-venomous snake, was never bothered by piranha (even though they occupied all streams), and only became ill briefly. On several occasions, he did receive painful and lingering insect bites. At night, he and other members of the party slept beneath a protective cover of mosquito netting. This precaution, however, was taken to protect against the fatal bite of rabid vampire bats as much as it was against insects.

As is true when traveling in any strange environment, the soon-to-be adventurer should learn as much as possible about his or her destination. Potential hazards should be identified and proper steps should be taken to avoid them. Away from the well-traveled tourist havens, the Wet Tropics can and often do offer discomforts such as heat, humidity, and swarms of biting insects. Few of the world's environments, however, offer a greater variety of life, natural beauty, or things of interest than does this fascinating region of the world.

5

Native Peoples

Tropical lands hold the oldest evidence of human existence. In fact, equatorial eastern Africa appears to have been humankind's original homeland. What factors may have contributed to our tropical origins? In fact, when we say "human," what do we mean? How have tropical peoples made their living and what, if anything, is unique about their way of life? Unlike stereotypes of "Tarzan-like" peoples living a meager "jungle" existence, life in the tropics has been and continues to be quite varied. This chapter attempts to answer such questions and to explain these and other fascinating aspects of tropical peoples past and present.

HUMAN ORIGINS IN TROPICAL AFRICA

Archaeologists (scientists who study early humans and their culture) believe that equatorial eastern Africa was the original homeland of mankind. This belief is strongly supported by a considerable body of evidence:

- Humans are large primates, and eastern Africa has the greatest number, variety, and size, as well as the longest history of primate species.

- Humans are tropical animals. When temperatures drop below 77°F (25°C), our bodies begin to feel the cold. Evidence suggests that tropical Africa was our home for at least half of human history. Only when we culturally developed survival techniques, such as control of fire, were we able to move beyond our tropical habitat into cooler areas.

- Numerous archaeological finds support the theory of a tropical African origin. Many of the significant discoveries were made by the famous Leakey family. For nearly seven decades, they searched for, found, and excavated many *Homo* species (human) remains. Their finds came from Tanzania's Olduvai Gorge and elsewhere within the region. Humans are *Homo* species, the remains of which date back several million years in eastern Africa.

- Equatorial eastern Africa offered a variety of physical conditions ideal for early humans. In the absence of distinct seasons, food and water were plentiful throughout the year. There was little need to protect against the cold. Few carnivorous predators such as lions or hyenas lived in the tropical rain forest, so early humans were relatively safe. Many volcanoes dot the region. They no doubt provided early humans with their first source of fire.

What Makes Humans Unique?

What does it mean to be "human"? *Homo sapiens* (modern humans) are primates, but so, too, are many other life-forms, including gorillas, chimpanzees, and monkeys. What separates us from them? We are like them in many ways, but different in others that are quite important when taken as a combination of factors. For example, we stand erect, freeing our hands and their opposable thumbs for work. We have three-dimensional eyesight and color vision. Humans are omnivorous, being able to digest both meat and plant material. Our brain is the largest in the animal world relative to body weight, and it is very complex. Our vocal apparatus allows us to make a wide range of sounds. Yet none of these factors, alone, makes us human.

Think for a moment about all those things that you possess that are not shared by other animals. Can you think ahead to what you will be doing a month from now, or reflect back on what you were doing a month ago? Of course! Other animals, scientist believe, do not have this ability. What really sets us apart from other species, therefore, is our ability to think and communicate abstractly. Most animals communicate, but the way they do it is determined by their biological makeup. That is, they are born with their language; it is not learned. Human communication must be learned. Because it is abstract, we can communicate ideas, share knowledge with others, and retain information about our past. You can read and understand the words on this page, learn from their content, and share what they say with others.

Humans also are highly creative in terms of their material culture. Look around you. How many things do you see that no other life-forms possess? All of these abilities and traits are a part of our *culture*, simply defined as learned human behavior. Humans, of course, apply their cultural ability in different ways. The result is a world divided into many different *cultures*, each of which has its own unique way of life. The abilities that we identify as "culture," and therefore the earliest human beings, first appeared in eastern Africa.

Race and Culture

It is extremely important to understand that race and culture are two totally different and unrelated concepts. Race refers to one's biological makeup; it is inherited and cannot be changed. Culture, as you now know, is our learned behavior. Race cannot be changed, but our culture changes rapidly. Race is a rather ambiguous and meaningless concept, one that is rarely used by scientists today. Nonetheless, many people still think in terms of racial classifications such as Negroid, Mongoloid, and Caucasoid. The distinctive physical features typically associated with each of these groups are quite recent developments in human evolution. None of them corresponds to the earliest humans who long ago migrated out of Africa. It is best to discard the idea of race as having any importance and think of peoples in terms of their cultural differences.

EARLY HUMAN MIGRATIONS

As was mentioned earlier, for perhaps half of human history, people were unable to move beyond the tropical environment. The earliest waves of people out of Africa may have followed the Nile River northward. During the ice age, environmental conditions were much different than they are today. For example, most of what today is the Sahara Desert was once quite wet. Many streams crossed the area, vegetation was plentiful, and grazing animals provided early hunters with food and skins for clothing and shelter. Outside of Africa, the earliest evidence of a human presence in the tropics points to Indonesia. There, on the island of Java, a skull aptly called "Java Man" (*Homo erectus*) has been dated to around 700,000 years ago.

Although the early migrations and earliest dates of human presence are interesting, they are of little importance geographically. With this in mind, we can leap ahead hundreds of thousands of years. Geographers, after all, are interested mainly in the migrations and ways of living practiced by different groups of humans (*Homo sapiens*). Certainly, by 50,000 years ago, all Old World (the Afro-Eurasian landmass) tropics were inhabited. It is now believed that Australia, too, had been reached by that date. (This migration, amazingly, would have involved at least some travel across open sea.)

How, when, and from where the earliest American peoples came remains one of the great unanswered human mysteries. Fifty years ago, scientists were sure they had the answers needed to fill in all the pieces of the First Americans puzzle. Most

The earliest known human resident of the tropics is the homo erectus Java Man, who was discovered by Dutch anatomist Eugène Dubois in 1891. Pictured here is a fossilized skull of a Java Man specimen on the island of Java, in Indonesia.

believed that big-game hunters from Asia crossed Beringia—the Bering Strait "Land Bridge" (a corridor linking Asia to present-day Alaska formed by the perhaps 400-foot [120-meter] drop in sea level during the last ice age). They then migrated through a supposedly ice-free corridor between two huge masses of glacial ice. Finally, they reached what is today the southwestern United States around 13,000 years ago.

Today, many scientists question this scenario. Some, in fact, boldly suggest a startling alternative theory. They believe that the earliest settlers may have come from different parts of the world by different routes and over a span of thousands of years. Tropical Southeast Asia, the islands of Japan, and frigid eastern Siberia have all been suggested as possible source areas; so have Europe, Africa, and even Australia. Had the earliest people come from the north (Beringia), it stands to reason that the oldest evidence should be found in northern North America. But it is not. Currently, the oldest generally accepted evidence of human habitation is in central and southern South America. What some scientists believe to be human footprints left 40,000 years ago were discovered recently in Mexico. A site in tropical eastern Brazil tentatively has been dated to 32,000 years ago.

We simply do not know when humans first arrived in the Americas. What is important is that some evidence of their earliest arrival places them in the tropics. There is also evidence to suggest that the earliest arrivals represented a variety of human physical types, including Negroid and Caucasoid, as well as the ultimately dominant Mongoloid. This suggests multiple migrations from different source areas, which almost certainly was the case. Such migrations, it is now believed, may have occurred by both land and water routes and over thousands of years. Despite the many lingering questions, it is apparent that most Native Americans came from Eastern Asia.

The Pacific islands were the last of the tropical lands to be reached and populated. Evidence suggests that some Melanesian and possibly Micronesian islands in the western Pacific were reached as early as 25,000 years ago. From this hearth area eventually occurred one of history's greatest seafaring accomplishments. By the time of Jesus Christ, nearly all tropical (and subtropical) Pacific islands had been discovered, and most had been settled by Polynesians. Two thousand years before Magellan's widely acclaimed voyage, these skilled sailors crossed thousands of miles of open sea. Their sturdy boats were huge, double-hulled canoes that were 100 feet (30 meters) or more in length. By the dawn of the Christian era, all of the world's tropical lands were settled.

EARLY CULTURES AND ECONOMIES

From the outset, the ways of life practiced by tropical peoples differed greatly. There were thousands of languages, belief systems, and patterns of social organization and interaction. Diets differed greatly; so did tools and means of protecting oneself against the natural elements (and often one's neighbors!). Knowledge, folklore, and art also varied. There also were many common elements shared by early humans. The list includes:

- **Dependence on local natural resources for survival**. In the tropics, plant and animal life, as well as water, were in abundance. The species did differ, however, from place to place. Through time, native cultures became very skilled in the use of local resources. Housing, clothing, tools, and weapons became well adapted to environmental conditions. Food, beverages, and a variety of organic medicines (many used by medical science today) also came from the natural surroundings.

- **Low populations and population densities**. For most of human history, the human population has been very low. Life expectancy was short, perhaps no more than 20-some years. Infant mortality was high, with many newly born youngsters dying at birth or before their first birthday. Populations also were widely scattered, with few people occupying an area. This practice prevented the land and resources from being pushed beyond their limit.

- **Minimal impact on the natural environment**. Because their numbers were low, early humans did not greatly change the environments in which they lived. This is particularly true of people living in the tropics. Fire, for example, has long been humankind's most useful tool in landscape change. In the tropics, however, it did not become a major factor until the beginning of slash-burn shifting cultivation. Major landscape changes in the tropics and elsewhere began with the dawn of agriculture.

- **Hunting-fishing-gathering economies**. Until the beginnings of agriculture, perhaps 10,000 to 15,000 years ago, all humans hunted and gathered in order to survive. Some also fished. Those living in the Wet Tropics had a decided advantage. With no seasons, nature provided a year-round abundance.

Men were the hunters. Their techniques varied greatly. Snares, nets, and traps were common. Some people became skilled users of bows and arrows; others depended on blow-

Shrunken Heads and a Cannibal Sea

At one time, a number of tropical tribal peoples were head-hunters, but only South America's Jívaro tribe also shrunk heads. These rain forest dwellers of eastern Ecuador believed that taking the head of an enemy would give them super-natural power.

The head of an enemy killed in battle was cut off. Skin was then removed from the skull, turned inside out, and carefully scraped. Mouth and eye openings were sewn shut, so the spirit of the deceased would be locked in and unable to seek revenge. The skin was then placed in a pot of water containing special plant extracts, and cooked. After several hours, it would shrink to about the size of a clenched fist. The shrunken head was then filled with hot sand until it dried. Finally, it was rubbed with preservatives. Needless to say, Europeans were horrified by this ghastly practice. As a traditional cultural ritual, killing enemies and shrinking their heads was discontinued more than a century ago. Today, heads for shrinking are taken from unclaimed cadavers in urban morgues, and the shrunken heads are sold only to museums.

And what about the "Cannibal Sea?" When early Spaniards arrived in the Caribbean region, they found some native peoples engaged in the ceremonial consumption of human flesh. Those peoples were called Caribs by the region's neighboring Arawak Indians. The Arawak term *Carib* means "cannibal." This name was adopted by the Spaniards. They used it not only in reference to the people, but also to the sparkling waters of the Caribbean—or Cannibal—Sea.

guns and their deadly poison-tipped darts. Women were gatherers. They collected roots, nuts, fruit, and berries. They also gathered "slow game," such as grubs, insects, snakes, eggs, small animals, and any other edible morsel found within their environment.

Fishing peoples also used a wide variety of techniques to make their catch. Nets, weirs, and spears or arrows were common. Hooks, too, were used, although less widely. Many types of piscicides (fish poisons) also were useful. In this practice, fish were attracted to calm water by some type of bait—perhaps a small nest of some insect and its larvae. Poisonous plant extracts were then placed in the water, either killing or stunning the fish.

AGRICULTURE BRINGS CHANGE

The world's cultures vary greatly in regard to their ways of living. Some cultures are highly developed and quite complex. They have many material possessions, live in communities, possess considerable knowledge, and share a rich vocabulary. Others cling to rather simple lifestyles and are very traditional in the way they live. How can such differences be explained? Through time, many hypotheses have been advanced, including conditions of the natural environment. Geographers, however, have long recognized that each of Earth's environments has been and continues to be home to an amazing array of cultures.

Life in the Wet Tropics is extremely diverse. It is impossible to speak of "tropical peoples," in the context of a homogeneous and environmentally influenced way of living. Some cultures, of course, do match the widely held stereotype. They continue to hunt, fish, and gather. Their lives, even today, differ little from those of all humans living several thousand years ago. Some tribal groups in the Amazon Basin remain very traditional. So, too, do the Pygmies living in the dense forests of the Congo Basin and various tribal peoples on the islands of Borneo, New Guinea, and elsewhere in Southeast

Among the tribal groups of the equatorial rain forests are the Pygmy, who are hunter-gatherers that live in Africa's Congo Basin. Pygmies are generally smaller than the average human, because they do not experience the growth spurt that typically occurs during the early teenage years.

Asia. Yet today within the region, many peoples' lives are as contemporary as yours and mine. In order to understand these differences, we must look to two great cultural events: the Agricultural Revolution and the Industrial Revolution (the importance of which is spotlighted elsewhere in this book).

The Dawn of Agriculture and Its Consequences

Where and when agriculture first began is not specifically known. Geographers and others recognize several "hearth" areas in which it seems to have first been practiced. Southwest Asia, Southeast Asia, and Mesoamerica (southern Mexico and Central America) appear to be among the earliest centers of plant domestication. Throughout human history, all people had gathered plant materials, rather than planting and harvesting crops. Perhaps 10 to 15 thousand years ago, this began to change. A few people (almost certainly women) began to deliberately plant and care for crops. This was the dawn of one of history's most important cultural revolutions.

With a greater and more reliable food supply, many changes began to occur. With more food, populations began to grow and life expectancy increased. Rather than constantly migrating, people could now settle in one place. Small communities began to grow. Houses became semipermanent habitations, allowing people to have more material possessions. With extended life expectancy, the elderly were able to share their knowledge and experience with their grandchildren. Some people became specialists—making pottery, baskets, or projectile points. Religious leaders were needed to keep social order and to ensure that the gods watched over their people and their crops and livestock. Strong young men were needed to protect the villages and fields from hostile neighbors. Someone, of course, had to pay for security. This meant taxes, which, in turn, required record keeping, systems of writing, and mathematics. These and other developments catapulted farming peoples far above those who continued to hunt and fish in terms of their level of cultural development.

From the original hearth areas, crop agriculture (and later animal domestication) diffused (spread) elsewhere. Soon farmers occupied much of tropical Central and South America, equatorial Africa, and Southeast Asia. Here, in the Wet Tropics, or immediately adjacent areas, several early civilizations emerged. In tropical (although not necessarily Wet Tropical) America, the Olmec, Mayan, and Inca civilizations flourished. Archaeologists are also beginning to find evidence of early high cultures in the Amazon Basin. In West Africa, several highly advanced kingdoms were supported by productive agricultural systems. The same is true of tropical portions of Southeast Asia.

Crops varied from region to region. In the American tropics, maize, sweet potatoes, manioc, and peanuts thrived; so did hot peppers, chocolate, and many fruits, including papaya and pineapple. Tropical Africa produced plantains (a cooking banana), bananas, yams, and coconut, among other crops. Southeast Asia specialized in rice, taro, bananas, citrus fruits, and sugarcane.

Traditional Farming in the Tropics

Traditional methods of tillage are quite similar throughout the world's Wet Tropics. The agricultural system must be well adapted to heavy rainfall and heavily leached, hence largely infertile, soils. Although recognized by many local terms, including the generic *swidden* or *shifting cultivation*, the author prefers using descriptive terminology. *Primitive slash-burn, shifting, subsistence farming* is a long term, but it defines the chief characteristics of this method of farming.

Techniques are traditional, hence, primitive by our standards. Tools are limited to the machete (a large, long, and heavy-bladed knife used for cutting and clearing), dibble (a pointed digging stick), and in some locations, the hoe. Forest vegetation is slashed using a machete and left to dry. Once

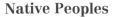

Slash-burn, or shifting cultivation, is a traditional farming method by which vegetation is first cut and then allowed to dry. After a certain amount of time (from a week to several months), the dry vegetation is burned and crops typically can be raised for one to five years before the plot must be moved.

dried, it is burned. Ash from the burned vegetation enters the soil as fertilizer. Most fields, however, remain littered with unburned stumps and the trunks of larger trees. Planting is somewhat random, a system of *intertillage*, in which crops are scattered about the plots, rather than in straight lines of homogeneous plants. Because soils rapidly become infertile, fields (and often villages) must shift from place to place every few years. Nearly half the deforestation occurring in tropical lands today is the result of this shifting form of cultivation. Finally, crops are grown only for subsistence. They are raised to feed a family, not for market.

Shifting cultivation is the world's most primitive type of farming, yet it provides us with several important cultural lessons. When judging other cultures and their practices, one must be extremely careful. In the United States, for example, soils throughout much of the South were ruined by unwise farming practices. Shifting cultivation, under normal conditions, is sustainable; that is, it can continue perpetually. Our agriculture system also is incredibly wasteful of energy: It takes more than 20,000 calories of energy to put 400 calories of food on a plate. Shifting cultivation, amazingly, is the world's most productive form of farming if measured by caloric energy produced in return for energy expended in production. In fact, it is the only type of farming that produces more energy than is put into planting, cultivating, and harvesting the crop.

Surprisingly, perhaps, no large animal domesticates came from the Wet Tropics. The South American llama and alpaca were limited to the high Andes. Cooler, drier upland areas of eastern Africa eventually became an area of cattle grazing. Cattle, however, are not native to the continent. Tropical Southern and Southeastern Asia did produce several domesticates. Water buffalo, zebu cattle, and poultry are native to the region (although not necessarily the Wet Tropics).

During recent centuries, great changes have come to the Wet Tropics. Much of the change has been imposed by midlatitude peoples who turned to tropical lands for raw materials, laborers, tropical agricultural products, and colonial expansion. The historical geography of European involvement with tropical lands and peoples is discussed in the next chapter.

6

European Influences

———◆———

Today, only a few of the world's most remote peoples have escaped the impact of spreading European culture and settlement. European exploration, exploitation, political control, and economic influences have reached the far corners of the world. Today, we think of those regions and peoples who have been reached by European culture as being "developed"; conversely, those areas less affected are often thought of as being "underdeveloped." In many respects, European influences have benefitted local peoples. In other ways, however, the impact of European contact has been detrimental. Native cultures have often been disrupted or even destroyed by the process of outside cultural contact.

Basically, the contacts between native and European peoples resulted in a clash of lifestyles, a collision of cultures—one very traditional and another quite advanced. The primary differences were those resulting from vast contrasts in the respective levels of technology and development. Europe was becoming increasingly industrial, commercial, urban, formally educated, and services oriented. The Wet Tropics (and many other places throughout the world at the time) remained dominantly rural and agrarian. Geographers often refer to the two ways of living as traditional *folk culture* and contemporary *popular culture.*

Throughout much of this chapter, the tropical world is divided into three regions: Tropical Latin America, equatorial Africa, and Southeast Asia, including Indonesia and adjacent islands. The historical geography of European influence unfolded in quite different ways in each of the three regions. In this chapter, attention is focused on events relating to European exploration, exploitation, and colonization in a historical context.

EARLY EUROPEAN EXPLORATION

Early Greeks believed that the tropical lands to their south were uninhabitable. From their midlatitude vantage point, they believed that people would simply burn up if exposed to the scorching tropical sun. By 425 B.C., however, the Greek historian and geographer Herodotus wrote (in disbelief) of a voyage that supposedly took place around 600 B.C. At about that time, an Egyptian king, Necho, supposedly sent an expedition of skilled Phoenician navigators southward along Africa's east coast. Three years later, they returned—by way of the Strait of Gibraltar and Mediterranean Sea—claiming to have sailed all the way around Africa. No one, of course, believed them! Among their claims, the most ridiculous was that when they sailed in the direction of the setting sun, the noonday sun appeared on their right (north). To northern midlatitude peoples, of course, such a claim served as further "proof" that reports of the voyage were a hoax. Now, of course, we know that this would, indeed, occur if they sailed around the southern tip of Africa. The assertion that cast greatest doubt on the voyage ultimately almost certainly proved that the voyage happened as reported by Herodotus.

Europeans had little tolerance for the high temperatures and humidity of the Wet Tropics. Of course, tropical peoples were much different than those with which they were familiar. And Europeans had little resistance to the many diseases that were so prevalent in tropical lands. For these and other reasons, it was not until the fifteenth century that European exploration of and contact with Wet Tropical lands got under way in earnest.

EUROPE LOOKS TO THE SEA

Much of the credit for early exploration by sea is given to Prince Henry ("The Navigator") of Portugal. Beginning in the early fifteenth century, Prince Henry developed a school of navigation at Sagres, located on the southwestern tip of Portugal. Shipbuilding, sail making, navigation, and other skills essential to making long voyages were taught. Soon, sailors from the school were traveling southward along Africa's Atlantic Coast. By the 1490s, ships were large and relatively safe, navigational skills were well honed, and the world was on the brink of one of its greatest events—the European Voyages of Discovery.

The story of sixteenth-century European exploration has been told many times. Basically, riches from the Orient—including silk from China and spices from the "Spice Islands" of Wet Tropical present-day Indonesia—were outlandishly expensive by the time they reached the Mediterranean Basin by land. Christopher Columbus is credited with the belief that the "East" could be reached by sailing westward across the Atlantic Ocean. Most Europeans of the time, including Columbus, believed the earth to be spherical (a reality that had been proved by Greeks nearly 2,000 years earlier). What they did not know was that a huge continental landmass lay between Europe and eastern Asia.

The Spanish Quest for Glory, God, and Gold

Columbus's epic voyage of 1492 reached the Antilles, islands of the Caribbean. It was not until his fourth voyage, in 1502,

Genoese explorer Christopher Columbus arrived in the New World when he landed at the Antilles on October 12, 1492. This painting depicts Columbus claiming the island, which he would rename San Salvador, or "Holy Savior."

that he actually set foot on the mainland of the Americas. The Spanish initially settled on the island of Hispañola in 1493, and, by 1511, they had settled all Caribbean islands on which gold was found: Cuba, Puerto Rico, Jamaica, and Trinidad. Spaniards, as is often noted, were in the New World seeking "glory, God, and gold." If gold was found, glory followed (at least for some). Catholic missionaries accompanied the Spanish explorers and early settlers. Conversion of native peoples was a primary objective of the Spanish Crown and Church. As it turned out, little gold was found by early Spanish explorers in the Wet Tropical region of Latin America.

Spaniards made many *entradas* (entrances) in Latin America, but with few exceptions, they skirted the tropics. Outside of the Caribbean islands, the only early Spanish settlement in the Wet Tropics was at Darien, in present-day Panama, founded in 1510. Being unaccustomed to the scorching heat and soggy humidity of the Wet Tropics, the Spaniards focused

Did Worms Play a Role in the Naming of America?

On his fourth voyage to the Americas in 1502 to 1504, Columbus found his ships' wooden hulls "badly worm eaten . . . and leaking alarmingly." The damage had been inflicted by a marine borer common to tropical waters, the toredo worm. Columbus and his crew were forced to put ashore for 11 days to make repairs on the vessels. Although some doubt remains in regard to the specific location, there is considerable evidence to suggest that it was along the Atlantic coast of Nicaragua.

There, Columbus and his crew found Indians adorned in gold jewelry and ornaments. It would be quite natural for the gold-hungry Spaniards to ask where the gold came from. The natives, no doubt, would have pointed inland to the source—then, as today, the *Amerique* (Americ, Amerrique) Mountains! Could word of this abundant source of gold in a land far across the Atlantic have reached mapmaker Martin Waldseemüller, who, in 1507, was the first to place the name "America" on a map?*

* For further information on this theory, see: Jorge Espinosa Estrada, *Nicaragua, Cuna de America* (Managua, Nicaragua: Editorial Alemana, 1969); Charles F. Gritzner, "Chickens, Worms, and a Little Bull: Some Animated Perspectives on American History," *Journal of Geography* 76:5 (March 1977): pp. 111–112.

their initial attention on settling Mexico (1519), Peru (1532), Ecuador (1535), Colombia (1536), Paraguay (1537), Chile (1540), Bolivia (1545), and Argentina (1580).

The earliest Spanish exploration of the Amazon Basin occurred in reverse—from headwaters to the river's mouth! In 1541, Francisco de Orellana and a small group were sent by Francisco Pizarro (the conqueror of Peru) down the eastern slope of the Ecuadorian Andes to search for gold. Once they descended the very steep, treacherous, and environmentally inhospitable slopes and entered the fast-flowing streams, they were unable to return to the highlands. They had no alternative but to follow the water routes that ultimately led them to the world's mightiest river—the Amazon. Little did they know that ahead stretched some 3,000 miles (4,800 kilometers) of water winding through the world's largest rain forest!

Along the Amazon, the Spaniards found many Indian groups. Some were hostile, armed with bows and poison-tipped arrows. During one heated encounter, Orellana lost an eye. According to some accounts, women were actively involved in the fighting against the strangers. Whether "Amazons" (fierce female warriors of Greek mythology) were actually involved in the fighting, or whether the Spaniards were duped by their own vivid imaginations, is unknown. Either way, however, an ancient legend born in the remote interior of Eurasia traveled across the Atlantic to give name to the world's greatest river: the Amazon. Orellana and the surviving members of his party reached Venezuela in 1542, becoming the first known people to cross the South American continent.

Portuguese in Brazil

In 1500—two years before Columbus set foot on the American mainland—Portuguese explorer Pedro Alvares Cabral reached the coast of Brazil. By the mid-sixteenth century, the Portuguese had lain claim to and established a foothold along the Wet Tropical coast of present-day Brazil. Unlike their Iberian neighbors, the Spanish, the Portuguese were interested in growing sugarcane, a crop that had been introduced to the Iberian Peninsula by Muslim Arabs early in the eighth century. The crop requires a warm, moist tropical climate and fertile soils. Coastal Brazil provided both.

By the late fifteenth century, Spanish interests clearly focused on the Americas and their rich gold (and later silver) deposits. Portuguese, on the other hand, were working their way down the Atlantic coast of Africa and had their sights set on reaching the Orient and its vast wealth. In 1494, a joint agreement was signed between the rulers of both countries that recognized these vastly different regional interests. A line of demarcation was established, which, in essence, gave Portugal free sailing in the waters of the eastern Atlantic, around Africa, and across the Indian Ocean to Asia. Spain claimed the western Atlantic and the Americas. This agreement, the Treaty of Tordesillas, would change through time, but its fundamental division remained primarily intact. The original line, located in the eastern Atlantic, ultimately was moved westward to recognize Portugal's interest in Brazil's coastal region.

Other Europeans

Other European powers also expressed interest in the Americas. The Dutch, French, and British established footholds in the Caribbean and along the northeastern tropical Guiana coastal region of South America. Initially, their primary interest was in preying upon Spanish vessels laden with gold en route to Spain. Piracy thrived in the Caribbean and to this day, many Spanish-founded cities—including San Juan, Puerto Rico (founded in 1521), and St. Augustine, Florida (founded in 1565)—have huge fortresses dating back nearly five centuries.

AFRICA: THE "DARK CONTINENT"

During the 1870s, American explorer Henry Morton Stanley gave Africa the nickname, "The Dark Continent." Ironically, this land lying so close to Europe was the last inhabited continent to be thoroughly explored by Europeans. The "darkness," therefore, existed in the lack of European knowledge of the lands and peoples who were located so near, yet in many ways so far away. Much of interior Africa, in fact, remained unseen by the European eye until the late decades of the nineteenth century. This is particularly true for Wet Tropical parts of the continent.

Portuguese navigators worked their way southward along Africa's Atlantic coast very gradually. By the mid-fifteenth century, they had reached the Guinea coastal area. It took nearly another half century, however, to round the Cape of Good Hope and timidly venture eastward into the waters of the Indian Ocean. Many factors help explain the very late penetration of Africa's interior. In the north, Europeans were repelled by the Sahara Desert, one of the world's great natural barriers. By the early eighth century, North Africa had become a Muslim stronghold and therefore a territory unfriendly to Christian Europeans. The African coast was treacherous, offering few places where European navigators could safely put ashore. Inland were dense forests, coastal marshes, and vast swamps. In addition, Europeans were accustomed to traveling by water, and most African rivers, including the mighty Congo and smaller Niger, have falls or rapids on their lower course. Europeans had no resistance to the many tropical diseases that they encountered. Unlike in the New World, no rich mineral stores were known to exist and little fertile soil was found. The greatest barrier to exploration, however, had nothing to do with environment. The Europeans found a far different source of wealth—human beings who were enslaved.

Unlike the early exploration of the Americas—that was driven by the search for wealth—much of the initial exploration of Africa was prompted by a sense of adventure and curiosity. Between 1795 and the time of his death in 1806, Mungo Park traveled widely in West Africa. The Scottish adventurer ultimately lost his life when his boat capsized while traversing rapids on the Niger River. Perhaps the best-known exploration of Africa's Wet Tropical interior region occurred between 1850

In 1869, Welsh-born American journalist Sir Henry Morton Stanley (pictured here) was sent to Africa by the owner of the *New York Herald* to find Scottish missionary and explorer David Livingstone. After two years traveling through central Africa, Stanley found the man who had been missing for six years on the shores of Lake Tanganyika, which lies on the border of present-day Burundi, Democratic Republic of the Congo, Tanzania, and Zambia.

and 1873. During this span of nearly a quarter century, another Scottish explorer, David Livingstone, traveled throughout much of central, southern, and eastern Africa. While traveling, Livingstone became ill and lost contact with the outside world for six years. In 1869, a New York newspaper sent Henry Morton Stanley to Africa in search of the lost explorer. The paper's publicity stunt was likened to the proverbial search for a "needle in a haystack." Yet after two years of wandering central Africa, amazingly, Stanley stumbled upon Livingstone in a small community on the shores of Lake Tanganyika. His greeting has gone down in history: "Dr. Livingstone, I presume?"

As had occurred centuries earlier in the American tropics, during the mid-to-late 1800s (after slavery had been outlawed), European powers other than the Portuguese began to express an interest in Africa. The British, French, and Dutch became involved, as did the Germans and Belgians.

SOUTHEAST ASIA'S "SPICE ISLANDS"

Southeast Asia's "Spice Islands"—the Malukus and other islands within present-day Indonesia—were a source of cloves, nutmeg, pepper, and other spices for many centuries before they were reached by European sailors. As early as 200 B.C., Arab traders may have reached the islands and begun a lucrative spice trade that ultimately reached European markets. Through time, cost became prohibitive for all but the wealthiest. Black pepper, for example, was more valuable than gold. Its value increased by up to 10,000 percent by the time it reached Mediterranean markets! It is little wonder that, by the late fifteenth century, Europeans began wondering if they, themselves, could become directly involved in the spice trade.

By 1511, Portuguese traders had reached Indonesia. A decade later, in 1521, Ferdinand Magellan, sailing under the Spanish flag, reached the Philippines. (Here, he was killed by natives, and so could not have been the first person to sail around the world.) In 1564, the Philippines became a Spanish colony, the first European holding in this part of the world. It was the Dutch, however, who would have the greatest impact on the islands. In 1596, several Dutch ships arrived at a port on the island of Java to take on a cargo of spices. So lucrative did this trade become, that many more Dutch vessels began making the long and dangerous journey. By 1602, these West Europeans were able to drive the British and Portuguese from the Spice Islands and with the formation of the Dutch East India Company, they began to monopolize the spice trade.

WINDS OF CHANGE SWEEP THE TROPICAL WORLD

As you have seen, different European powers each had their own interests in the tropics. In the Americas, the Spanish feverishly sought gold, whereas the Portuguese were happy to find a land suitable for growing "white gold," sugarcane. Throughout much of tropical Africa, both exploration and European impact came late. Once Europeans became involved in the African slave trade—begun in earnest by the Portuguese during the mid-fifteenth century—other interests in the continent rapidly waned. The Belgians became established in the Congo Basin, and the British and French gained footholds in most of Wet Tropical West Africa. They also had holdings in the Caribbean and on South America's Guiana coast. In Southeast Asia, the Dutch soon claimed much of the region and its lucrative spice trade. Winds of cultural change were about to sweep across the lands and peoples of the Wet Tropical realm.

EUROPEAN EXPLOITATION AND SETTLEMENT

European exploitation of the Wet Tropics has occurred only during the past five centuries, and throughout much of the realm's three regions, settlement has been temporary. As you have seen, people have been drawn to the tropics for a variety of reasons. Most "invaders" have been lured by the hope of profiting from resources—minerals, soils, plants, and in Africa, humans. Others came (usually reluctantly) as government administrators, military personnel, or for some other political or strategic reason. Very few came to make a home and stake their future in this region. To Europeans, it was an alien environment, one that was oppressively hot and humid, rife with diseases against which they had no immunity, and inhabited by natives with strange cultures and customs.

As recently as the mid-twentieth century, the tropics were looked upon by many as being a "White Man's Grave." This perception seems strange, inasmuch as the tropics are the environment to which all humans are physically best adapted. No race of people appears to be better or worse suited, biologically, to the tropical (or any other) environment. Further, about 10 percent of all humans live in humid tropical lands. Clearly, we must look to some other factor(s) for an explanation. The answer lies in what geographers call "environmental perception." Fundamentally, most of us simply do not want to live in areas that are extremely hot and humid and where weather is marked by extreme monotony. Of even greater importance is culture. Many tropical areas simply lack the amenities and comforts to which we are accustomed—shopping, entertainment, sanitation facilities, good schools, adequate medical facilities, and, yes, even air-conditioning. Where these things are found, so, too, are substantial numbers of people of European (including American and Canadian) ancestry. Nonetheless, throughout most of the Wet Tropical region, people with midlatitude roots remain in a very small minority, usually no more than a percent or two of the population.

When midlatitude peoples did find themselves living in the tropics, it was usually for a short term. In the Americas, many were colonial government administrators, some managed plantations and other economic enterprises, still others came to prospect for wealth. Missionaries came to save souls. In most locations, a military presence was necessary to protect Europeans and their interests. Some came simply to escape or to seek adventure. In French Guiana, some 80,000 came as criminals, assigned to the infamous "Devil's Island" penal colony. By assigning white prisoners to their Wet Tropical colony in northeastern South America, the French hoped to achieve two goals. First, they hoped to rid the homeland of undesirables; second, they hoped to establish the world's only dominantly white colony in the tropics. The experiment proved to be a dismal failure. More than 90 percent of all prisoners died, most within a year or two of their arrival.

In Africa, nearly all European colonial settlement hugged the coast. Initially, this pattern of settlement resulted from the nature of the slave trade in which local tribesmen delivered captured slaves to coastal ports. Later, the seafaring-oriented European exploiters and colonizers continued to cling to coastal locations because of cooling sea breezes and easy access to shipping lanes. The primary exceptions were in East Africa, where Europeans established colonial capitals in the cooler tropical highlands. Mining and tropical plantations, as well as the infrastructure needed to maintain their colonies and businesses, were the primary magnets that drew Europeans to tropical Africa. As in Latin America, missionaries, military personnel, and a few adventurers also had a presence in the region. Some came to help the African people. Dr. Albert Schweitzer, a German-born physician, opened a hospital in Lambaréné, Gabon, in 1913 that he continued to staff until his death in 1965. For his humanitarian efforts, Dr. Schweitzer received the 1952 Nobel Peace Prize.

The pattern was quite similar in Southeast Asia. A small number of French were involved on the mainland in what then was French Indo-China, and the Dutch were active in the trade of spices, tropical hardwoods, and later rubber in Indonesia. There was one major exception: Unlike in Latin America and tropical Africa, Christian missionaries made little headway among the dominantly Muslim population of Indonesia. The Philippines, under Spanish control until 1898, when they were ceded to the United States after the Spanish-American War, became 80 percent Roman Catholic. The Spanish presence in this island country was somewhat stronger than that of

German-born physician Albert Schweitzer was awarded the 1952 Nobel Peace Prize for founding the Lambaréné hospital in Gabon. Schweitzer established the hospital in 1913, which he used to treat hundreds of patients who suffered from leprosy and African sleeping sickness.

other European colonizers. For 250 years (1565 to 1815), the Spaniards maintained a lucrative trade between their colony and Mexico. The famous Manila Galleons carried spices and other tropical goods from the Philippine capital to Acapulco on Mexico's Pacific coast.

THE COLONIAL LEGACY

In summary, the European physical and cultural presence in the Wet Tropics is quite minor when compared with that of former midlatitude colonies (including those of the United States, Canada, and Australia). Nonetheless, throughout the Wet Tropics, some impact of European presence is evident—in some places hardly visible, in others quite evident. Within the tropics, only two countries—Liberia in West Africa and Thailand in peninsular Southeast Asia—were never colonized by European powers.

Elsewhere, the former colonizer's cultural imprint is evident in a number of ways. Spanish, French, and English (among others) are the official tongue in many countries. With the exception of Southeast Asia (other than the Philippines), Christianity gained a widespread following. Many customs remain firmly in place, such as afternoon tea in former British colonies and wine with meals in former French-held lands. Architecture and customs often show a direct link, as do diets and systems of government.

Whether, in the long run, colonization was good or bad for native peoples remains a controversial issue eliciting sharply differing opinions. Certainly, tropical peoples were exposed to midlatitude culture, including technology, medical advances, a cash economy, and ideas of human equality and democracy. We can only imagine what the way of life might be in remote tropical lands had contact with European culture never occurred. In this context, it is important to remember that independence occurred at different times and over a span of more than a century.

Some historians suggest that a correlation exists between long ago versus recent independence. This line of thinking suggests that the longer a former colony has been independent, the better off it should be. Under close scrutiny, this theory simply does not stand in the light of historical reality. As was mentioned previously, Liberia was never colonized, yet it is a very poor and troubled land. In the Caribbean, Haiti gained its independence from France in 1804, more than two centuries ago, to become the world's first black-controlled independent country. Today, Haiti is one of the world's poorest and politically least stable countries. Most Latin American countries gained independence from Spain (or Brazil from Portugal) between 1820 and 1840. Indonesia gained independence in 1949, whereas much of tropical Africa was not freed of the colonial yoke until the 1960s.

Colonization did, of course, have a negative side against which few could argue convincingly. It created a highly stratified society in which Europeans dominated a largely poor and powerless native population. European "ways" of doing things were unquestionably the "right" ways. Because of this hierarchy, native peoples rarely were well educated and few gained experience in running businesses, providing essential services, or governing. Much of the postindependence trouble experienced in so many former colonies can be attributed to this lack of preparation. Vast wealth was taken from colonial holdings, with little benefit to native peoples. In Africa, problems resulting from the European-imposed political boundaries have proven to be all but impossible to surmount. After gaining independence, there was a widespread desire to rid the country of colonial influences. As a result, many countries (particularly in Africa) took huge steps backward in terms of development on the Western model.

Some common criticisms are unfair. For example, there is a widely held belief that the development of tropical plantations displaced native landholders and subsistence farmers. Little evidence exists, however, to support this belief. Most native peoples in the tropics lived in cooler, healthier, upland interior areas, where they practiced shifting cultivation. Few coastal plains were inhabited. You will recall from the discussion of tropical soils in Chapter 3 that most are quite infertile. Along coastal plains, however, water deposited alluvial soils are fertile. Obviously, soil fertility is a prime factor in deciding where to place a multimillion dollar agricultural investment! This misconception no doubt results from the fact that, once a plantation is established, many native peoples move into the area. Jobs become available, disease-spreading insect populations are reduced, and transportation facilities are improved. Towns with schools and hospitals are built, and many other amenities are introduced, all of which tend to draw native peoples to the coastal environment. In the following chapter, we will assess present-day conditions throughout the Wet Tropical realm and its three subregions.

7

Contemporary Conditions and Regions

During recent decades, a number of terms and concepts have been developed in reference to the world's poorest countries and peoples. *Underdeveloped, less developed, developing,* and *third-world* are among the designations—all of which point to a central theme: poverty. In this context, it is extremely important to consider once again the cultural differences described in the preceding chapter, particularly the distinction between folk and popular culture. When people accustomed to Western culture think "poor," we really are thinking "non-Western," or, more specifically, people sharing a noncommercial, self-sufficient, folk culture. *Wealth* and *poverty* are relative terms that have meaning only in the context of a specific culture. That is to say, someone we may consider to be dirt poor may, in the eyes of his community, be extremely well-to-do.

Using the economic indicators most frequently employed by economists and such international bodies as the World Bank and United Nations, the region is marked by widespread poverty.

Per-capita income, gross domestic product, gross national product, and purchasing power parity all generally rank well below world averages.

ECONOMIC ACTIVITIES

In the hierarchy of economic activity—primary, secondary, and tertiary—primary industries continue to dominate the economy of tropical lands. Only in a few places, such as Singapore, Hawaii, and the Caribbean islands of Barbados and Puerto Rico, do service industries dominate. Throughout most of the region, mineral extraction, agriculture, and logging, and in some locations fishing, are the most important economic activities.

Primary (Extractive) Industries

Mineral extraction has long been important to economies throughout much of the tropical world. Today, we continue to look to these lands for many important metals and fuels. Rich iron deposits are being mined in Brazil, Venezuela, and Liberia. The Democratic Republic of the Congo and Indonesia produce copper, whereas Brazil, Nigeria, Malaysia, and Indonesia are major producers of tin. Bauxite, the ore from which aluminum is made, is mined in Jamaica, Guyana, Suriname, several West African countries, and Malaysia. Petroleum is the most important export of Indonesia, Venezuela and Ecuador, and several countries in western equatorial Africa, including Nigeria. Gabon has major deposits of uranium.

Plantation agriculture is the economic lifeblood of many tropical countries. Coffee, alone, is the leading export of about 40 countries, most of which are located in the tropics. Many important crops are plantation grown. Food crops include coconuts, bananas, cacao (chocolate), sugarcane, pineapples (and other tropical fruits), spices, and, of course, coffee and tea. Industrial crops raised on plantations include rubber, palm oils, and jute (a fiber crop). Plantations depend upon a formula of two "L's" and three "M's": Land and labor are both local, but the midlatitudes provide markets, money (capital for develop-

Many tropical countries rely on plantation agriculture to support their economies. The most important fruit crop is the banana, which is grown in 130 countries worldwide and ranks fourth in human consumption behind rice, wheat, and maize. Pictured here is a man harvesting bananas on a Chiquita plantation near Siquirres, Costa Rica.

ment and operation), and management. Because of tropical soil conditions, most plantations are in coastal regions. They dot the coast of Brazil, Central America, Guyana, and many Caribbean islands. Plantations also are numerous along the east-west–extending coastal plain of West Africa. In Indonesia and the Philippines, rich soils of volcanic origin allow plantations to move inland.

Livestock ranching is a rather recent tropical endeavor, but one that has experienced rapid growth since the development of effective refrigeration. Until the development of artificial cooling, meat would spoil rapidly in the hot, humid, fly-infested tropical environment. Today, however, the beef in the hamburger you had for lunch may well have come from a steer raised in Central America or Brazil's Amazon Basin. Most breeds of cattle are poorly adapted to humid tropical conditions. Tropical African and Asian cattle, such as the humped Zebu (Brahman), however, survive well in hot, humid conditions.

Logging is gaining in importance throughout most of the tropical realm, and often with severe environmental consequences, as described in Chapter 4. Most deforestation results from a desire to simply clear the land of trees so it can be used for other purposes. Only in a few locations, such as the Indonesian islands of Borneo and New Guinea, are huge areas being cut over for the timber, itself. Clearly, deforestation is becoming a global, rather than local, environmental issue, and solutions to the problem beg international cooperation and resolve.

Harvesting marine resources is primarily of local importance. Throughout much of the tropical world, fish taken from rivers, lakes, or the sea provide the primary source of protein. Commercially, tropical waters are not a primary source of commercial species. However, much of the shrimp sold in American markets is artificially grown in lands as far apart as Ecuador and Thailand.

Secondary (Processing and Manufacturing) Industries

Throughout most of the tropical world, manufacturing is limited to the production of basic needs for local consumption. Matches, building materials, beverages (beer and soft drinks), clothing and footwear, hunting and fishing gear, and simple agricultural implements are usually locally made. So, too, are some food products. The internationalization of manufacturing was amply illustrated to the author recently. He purchased three shirts, all having the same brand-name label. Yet they had been manufactured in Costa Rica, Thailand, and the Philippines!

Other than with plantations, midlatitude investors have been slow to risk their capital in most tropical countries. Industrial development is hindered by several factors. Many tropical countries lack a skilled labor force. In some areas, in fact, the idea of working for wages (to people accustomed to a traditional subsistence economy based on barter exchange) is totally alien to their experience. Political instability, inept and corrupt local bureaucracies, and the lack of adequate infrastructure further discourage foreign investment. Creation of a viable business involves much more than the mere building of a manufacturing plant! Very little manufacturing for export exists in the American or African tropics. Southeast Asia has been somewhat more successful in this regard.

Tertiary (Service) Industries

Tertiary industries are those that provide some kind of direct service to consumers. Examples include education, entertainment, financial services, health care, insurance, or any commercial activity associated with travel and tourism. In this context, it is important to keep in mind the nature of an economic system. Systems are interrelated activities or units. Think, for a moment, about how many interacting components there are to the tourism industry. Tourists must get to a destination, either by a combination of air, ship, rail, local public transportation, or car rental. Car rental, alone, involves agencies, insurance, service, gas stations, maps, and much more. Lodging facilities and restaurants are needed to house and feed visitors. Many travelers in a foreign land—particularly one offering a "foreign" culture—want packaged tours. The destination must offer natural, historical, or cultural attractions. Above all, travelers want to know that they are safe from criminal acts, disease, and other hazards. Tourism, as you can see, is extremely complex and can involve billions of investment dollars.

Despite its complex and costly nature, tourism offers the best hope for economic development for much of the tropical world. Throughout most of the region, tourism began coming to some locations with the onset of the jet age. This is true for many islands in the Caribbean and certainly is the case for most tourist destinations in the Pacific and Indian oceans. Prior to the 1960s, once incredibly remote vacation spots, such as Hawaii and Fiji, Jamaica and Barbados, or Bali and Phuket, were rarely visited. Today, each of these locations is a major tourist destination.

Would you like to visit the tropics? Certainly, most of us would! They have much to offer environmentally, historically, and culturally. Would you prefer, though, to go to Hawaii or Africa's equatorial Guinea? If your answer is "the African country," perhaps you are either a geographer or think like one! Most readers, however, almost surely would opt for the tropical "paradise" of Hawaii. There, they would find all facilities, services, attractions, and amenities needed to make their visit safe and pleasurable.

Perhaps more so than any other single factor, the percentage of working-age people engaged in service industries provides a valid index of a country's economic development. Throughout most of the tropical world, less than half of the working population is engaged in this sector of the economy. In most of tropical Africa, fewer than a quarter of the people are so employed. In Nigeria, the region's leading economic power, only about 25 percent of workers are engaged in service-related tasks. Even in economically advanced Singapore, the figure stands at about two-thirds, the same as in rapidly developing Brazil. At the other extreme, on several Caribbean Islands (for example, the Cayman Islands and Barbados), nearly all employed people are involved in service industries.

Returning to the extreme cost and complexity of developing an economic system, some correlations stand out. In countries with low levels of literacy, short life expectancies, poor governments, high crime rates, and low per-capita incomes, a very low percentage of working-age people are involved in service industries. Just the opposite is true for lands with the majority of their people providing services. Recently, the author had a problem with his computer. He called the firm's 1-800 service number, reached an agent, and spent more than an hour trying to resolve the problem. When asked where the young service representative was located, the answer was, "Manila, in the Philippines."

With instantaneous global communication networks in place and improving educational opportunities throughout much of the tropical world, might this experience provide a hint of future opportunities and development?

POPULATION CHARACTERISTICS

The Wet Tropics is home to about 10 percent of the world's population, or about two-thirds of a billion people. Within the region, however, some remarkable extremes occur in terms of population, settlement, density, and a variety of other demo-graphic conditions. For example, Indonesia (246 million) and Brazil (188 million) are the world's fourth- and fifth-ranking countries in terms of population. Nigeria (132 million), much of which lies within the Wet Tropics, ranks tenth. Scattered throughout the region are also some of the world's smallest countries, in terms of both size and the number of people who call them home. Tiny Nauru, a mere dot in the Pacific Ocean, is a country with an area of only 8 square miles (21 square kilo-meters) and a population of about 13,000. Another tropical Pacific island country, Pitcairn, has only about 50 people!

Settlement and Density

A glimpse of the population map quickly reveals that, within the Wet Tropics, people are not evenly distributed. Huge areas support very low populations. Much of the Amazon and Congo basins, huge areas roughly half the size of the United States, have a density of fewer than two people per square mile (one per square kilometer). On the other hand, some of

Singapore is an island city-state located in Southeast Asia and is the second-most densely populated country in the world (18,000 people per square mile). The city is pictured here from Boat Quay, which is located on the Singapore River in the southern part of the city.

the world's highest population densities also are found in Wet Tropical lands. Obviously, people can and do live in the Wet Tropics, and populations can thrive in hot, humid environments. The Indonesian island of Java has an area about the size of Alabama, yet it is home to about 124 million people. The island's density is one of the world's highest, with more than 2,500 people per square mile (980 per square kilometer). In tiny Singapore, the density rises to nearly 18,000 per square mile (6,930 per square kilometer).

How can such huge differences in numbers and density of people be explained? This is not an easy question to answer, because each location is somewhat unique. Basically, people tend to live where they can make a living—whether hunting, fishing, and gathering at one extreme, or working for wages at the other. Many factors determine an area's potential productivity. They include the environment itself, cultural adaptation to environmental conditions, human perceptions of environment, and available capital resources and technology. A tropical island, for example, may have few natural resources and little industry, but a great deal of natural beauty. People thousands of miles away with money to travel may be attracted to the place by its solitude, scenery, and "quaint" culture. This alone, however, is not enough. People must have the time, money, and desire to travel. Speedy jet aircraft must be available to move them swiftly to their desired destination. In addition, an adequate tourist infrastructure—hotels, restaurants, service personnel, and other amenities—must exist before the island can become a prime tourist destination. As on a number of tropical islands, with tourism, native peoples thrive economically, and the population grows.

In other locations, such as the aforementioned Amazon and Congo basins, access is difficult, jobs are scarce, and few towns and other amenities exist. People simply are not attracted to such areas in large numbers.

Demographic Conditions

It is always hazardous to generalize, because exceptions always occur. For the region as a whole, however, the following general conditions prevail in terms of demographics. Throughout most of the region, for example, birthrates are well above the world average, and in tropical Africa they are more than double the global figure. Death rates, too, rank among the world's highest. Yet, surprisingly, perhaps, much of the region also experiences the world's leading rate of natural population increase (RNI). In equatorial Africa, for example, every country exceeds the world RNI average, most by a considerable margin. In Congo and the Democratic Republic of the Congo, the population is growing at a rate almost three times greater than the current world average of 1.2 percent per year.

Throughout most of the region, life expectancy drops far below that of the developed world—by a whopping 20 to 25 years in much of the region. Because of high birthrates and high death rates, the population tends to be young. In many tropical countries, 40 to 45 percent of the population is under 15 years of age! In addition, most of the population remains rural, poorly educated, and poverty-stricken.

Despite these gloomy figures, there are some remarkable success stories scattered throughout the Wet Tropics. Caribbean islands such as Martinique, Guadalupe, and Barbados far outrank world averages and even many developed countries, in most if not all demographic categories. So does the Central American republic of Costa Rica. In Southeast Asia, Singapore and Thailand claim demographic figures that would be the envy of many industrialized Western countries.

GOVERNMENT

Perhaps the single most important key to a country's success or failure is its government. History has proven time and time again that good government provides the foundation for economic growth and other conditions that contribute to human well-being. Unfortunately, political stability and good government are rare exceptions, rather than the general rule, throughout the region. Although most countries claim to be democratic, few have really achieved a level of stability and equality in the eyes of the law that Northern Americans take for granted.

In fact, during recent decades, open conflict has beset countries in all three subregions. It continues today in some areas. In the American tropics, Haiti and Ecuador have a long history of turmoil. In Cuba, Fidel Castro has held an iron (and Communist) grip on island politics for nearly a half century. Over the years, politics have been turbulent in Guyana and Suriname and none too stable in Jamaica. In Africa, it is much more difficult to identify the tropical lands that enjoy relatively good governments. Only two—Ghana and Cameroon—stand out in this regard. Some African states, including Nigeria, are on the brink of becoming ungovernable, according to some observers. In Southeast Asia, political turmoil is the rule, rather than the exception. Until such time as honesty, integrity, democratic rule, and stability become the political order of the day, most countries within the region will continue to languish economically and people living there will continue to suffer. Sadly, most countries within the region have a long way to go. A perusal of the *Human Development Index* and *Corruption Perceptions Index* (both can be accessed online using a search engine) is revealing. Most countries languishing at or near the bottom of both indexes are located within the Wet Tropics.

SUBREGIONS OF THE WET TROPICS

It is easy to hold stereotypes about people living in a particular natural environment, in this case, of course, "tropical people." This approach, however, can be extremely misleading. A student in Honolulu, Hawaii, Singapore, or Bridgetown, Barbados, will spend the day doing much the same things as you will be doing. Yet in remote areas of the Amazon and Congo basins, some tribal peoples still cling to a Stone Age culture. The same holds true for some groups inhabiting isolated islands of Indonesia, the Philippines, and Papua New Guinea. What inhabitants of this realm do share in common is that they have all learned to live comfortably in a Wet Tropical environment. The final section of this chapter presents a brief contemporary overview of the three major subregions within the tropical world and the scattered islands within the Pacific and Indian oceans.

The American Tropics

More than 90 percent of the American tropics lie within the equatorial portion of South America, mainly in the vast Amazon Basin. Small outlying areas include the isolated and sparsely populated Pacific coast of Colombia, eastern lowlands of Central America, and windward (northeastern) portions of some islands in the eastern Caribbean.

The Chocó coast of Colombia is the wettest area on mainland America. Backed by towering peaks of the northern Andes, the area is also extremely remote. Only one road reaches the coast from the interior highlands. It winds its way down the mountain slopes from Cali to Buenaventura, Colombia's only port on the Pacific Ocean. Once a remote, sleepy backwater, today Buenaventura is a bustling city of about 300,000 people.

Central America has long held the nickname, "The Banana Republics," and with good reason. Since the late 1800s, the

The Panama Canal

The Panama Canal crosses the narrow Isthmus of Panama to link the Atlantic and Pacific oceans. When built by the U.S. Army Corps of Engineers from 1904 to 1914, the canal was one of the largest and most difficult construction projects ever undertaken. The hazardous project was plagued by many problems. Deadly malaria and yellow fever, along with massive and frequent mudslides, took the lives of an estimated 27,500 workers.

When opened in 1914, the roughly 50-mile (80-kilometer) long canal cut nearly 8,000 treacherous miles (12,900 kilometers) off a voyage from San Francisco to New York City around Cape Horn at the southern tip of South America. Each year, about 14,000 ships, or nearly 40 a day, make the short passage through the canal's six major locks and Lake Gatun. The freshwater lake serves as a filter that prohibits the passage of marine organisms between the two oceans.

In 1977, President Jimmy Carter signed an agreement to transfer the canal to Panama by the end of 1999. Since that tropical lowlands bordering the Caribbean Sea have been the world's foremost area of commercial banana production. Today, corporations such as Dole, Chiquita, and Del Monte control much of the production. From the highlands come some of the world's finest coffee beans, including Guatemalan Antigua and Costa Rican Tarrazú. Central America holds huge potential for development of the tourist industry. It is close to the United States and offers marvelous scenery, a rich history, and a fascinating mosaic of native cultures. Cities include Belize City and Belmopan (Belize), San Salvador (El Salvador), Guatemala City (Guatemala), Tegucigalpa (Honduras), Managua (Nicaragua), San José (Costa Rica),

time, operations have continued to function smoothly under Panamanian control.

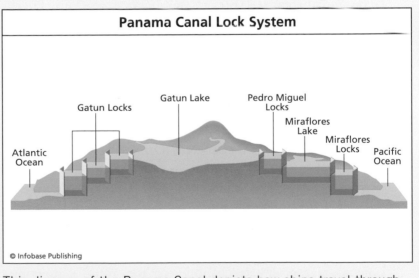

Panama Canal Lock System

Gatun Lake

Gatun Locks

Pedro Miguel Locks

Miraflores Lake

Miraflores Locks

Atlantic Ocean

Pacific Ocean

© Infobase Publishing

This diagram of the Panama Canal depicts how ships travel through the waterway that connects the Atlantic and Pacific oceans.

and both Colón and Panamá (Panama). Although each city has some industrial development and offers a variety of services, only San José and Belize City have developed as significant tourist destinations. Throughout the last half of the twentieth century, much of the region was embroiled in civil conflicts that discouraged economic development of any kind. Now relatively stable, the region can look ahead with some optimism to a better future.

Caribbean Islands

Technically, most of the Caribbean region experiences a seasonal wet-and-dry tropical climate. Most Northern Americans, however, are unconcerned about this scientific distinction. Canadians and Americans alike flock to the Caribbean to enjoy a "tropical" vacation. Culturally, the islands offer a rich tapestry of native, African, and European culture that, of course, has become extremely mixed on most islands. Because the islands were all colonized by European powers, they also offer a mixture of Spanish, British, French, and Dutch cultures, as well.

Politically, much of the region is quite stable. Communist Cuba and turbulent Haiti are the major exceptions. Puerto Rico, which enjoys Commonwealth status within the United States, has a bustling economy. Although on a much smaller scale, a number of smaller islands are doing quite well economically. Martinique and Guadeloupe are departments of France (holding the same status as does a state in the United States or province in Canada), and the prosperity resulting from this affiliation is very evident to the traveler.

Barbados and the Cayman Islands, too, are doing extremely well financially. Tourism thrives throughout much of the region. Plantation agriculture featuring bananas and sugarcane, as well as limited manufacturing, also boost the economy of some islands. The islands also export popular culture: Calypso, reggae, and steel band music, for example, are popular throughout much of the world.

South American Wet Tropics

With the exception of coastal plantations in Guyana and Brazil, development of South America's vast area of Wet Tropics has come very slowly. Although the alluvial floodplain of the mighty Amazon stretches out as much as 50 miles (80 kilometers) along both sides of the river, this fertile area floods regularly. Some half century ago, the Brazilian government decided to do what it could to encourage settlement in, and development of, the Amazon Basin. Two decisions, in particular, had a remarkable effect.

First was the decision in 1966 to make the sleepy central Amazonian community of Manaus a free (tariff-free) port. The city is actually located on the Rio Negro, about 11 miles (18 kilometers) upstream from its juncture with the Amazon. Oceangoing ships can easily navigate the 900 miles (1,450 kilometers) upstream to Manaus (actually, they can reach Iquitos, in eastern Peru). This move proved to be very successful. During the past four decades, the population of the city and surrounding area swelled from about 100,000 to nearly 2 million. In addition to its port and trade functions, Manaus has become the Amazon Basin's chief manufacturing center. Shipbuilding, brewing, chemicals, electronic equipment, and petroleum refining (of oil transported by barge from Peru) are among the local industries. A thriving tourist industry—particularly ecotourism for people wanting to experience the rain forest environment—has developed during recent decades.

Second was the decision to build the Trans-Amazonian Highway. This ambitious project was initially designed to cross the continent, linking eastern Brazil with Ecuador and Peru. Later, that idea was dropped, and the road was planned to stretch about 2,000 miles (3,200 kilometers), from Recife westward to Rio Blanco, an isolated city in Acre, Brazil's westernmost state. From the very outset, in the early 1970s, the project met with only partial success. Most of the road was unpaved and impassable due to recurrent flooding. Settlers

The Brazilian city of Rio de Janeiro is best known for its Carnival, which is held each year right before the season of Lent. Pictured here are the Carnival King and Queen during the opening ceremonies of the 2005 Carnival.

who followed the road inland—with dreams of land ownership and prosperity—soon learned what scientists had long known, that most tropical soils are infertile. Meanwhile, vast areas of dense rain forest were cleared and perhaps lost forever. Today, much of the road is still impassable. The Amazon River and its tributaries, and expensive air travel, remain the primary means of transportation throughout the Amazon Basin.

Most Brazilians live along the tropical coast, which extends from Rio de Janeiro northeastward to Fortaleza and includes the cities of Salvador and Recife. This area has long been a major producer of sugar (from cane). Today, the economy is diversifying, with industry, services, and tourism all becoming increasingly well developed, and Brazil's economy is now booming. Rio de Janeiro, located at the edge of the Wet Tropics, remains one of the world's most spectacular and dynamic urban centers. The thriving city of some 6 million is perhaps best known for its annual Carnival celebration, held in conjunction with Mardi Gras each (Southern Hemisphere) summer.

Wet Tropical Africa

Fortune has not been kind to much of Wet Tropical Africa during recent decades. Few areas of the world, in fact, have undergone more turbulence and hardship. Within the region, only Ghana and Cameroon have a history of political stability, and both countries are doing relatively well. Côte d'Ivoire is the world's leading producer of cacao. During recent years, however, this once stable former French colony has undergone considerable internal conflict.

The largest tropical West African country—in area, population, and economy—is Nigeria. It is also one of the most troubled. This oil-rich nation is divided between Christian and Animist peoples in the south and Muslims in the north. They differ not only in religion, but also in language and many other aspects of culture. Politically, the country is extremely unstable and, in the judgment of many, on the brink of becoming ungovernable.

In Central Africa, with the exception of Cameroon, oppressive governments, grinding poverty, widespread corruption, and tragic conflicts have reigned. Nowhere have things been worse than in the eastern portion of the Democratic Republic of the Congo (DRC) and neighboring Rwanda and Burundi. In 1994, after several decades of tension-building between Tutsi and Hutu tribesmen, civil war exploded in Rwanda. Tutsi rebels "won," resulting in more than a million Hutus seeking refuge in neighboring countries. Hostilities spilled over into Uganda and the DRC, leaving those already impoverished nations in even further turmoil. Although the exact figure will never be known, it is believed that as many as one million people may have lost their lives directly or indirectly because of this heated conflict.

Wet Tropical Africa is home to an estimated 270 million people. Its coastal plains and river valleys offer an abundance of fertile soil. The region is rich in petroleum resources and hydroelectric potential. Several countries have substantial deposits of iron ore, copper, and other metals. A combination of environmental, historical, and cultural attractions has the potential to draw tourists to the region. Unfortunately, a host of factors discourage tourism and most other developmental potentials. Inept governments, continuing intertribal hostilities, endemic corruption, widespread poverty, and inadequate infrastructure are among the many conditions that make it difficult to look ahead with much optimism for this part of the world.

Southeast Asia

Nowhere in the Wet Tropics has development occurred at a faster recent pace than in Southeast Asia. As author Douglas Phillips noted in his book *Southeast Asia*, "Today, the importance of the Southeast Asian culture realm is ever present. It may be found in the shrimp you eat, the clothes you wear, the computer you use, or the ancestry of a close friend." Here, in Malaysia's capital city, Kuala Lampur, you will find the world's tallest building—the Petronas Twin Towers—a fitting symbol of the recent economic boom enjoyed in this peninsular country and throughout much of Southeast Asia.

World attention focused on this region, known for its many natural hazards, on December 26, 2004. On that date, a giant earthquake occurred in the Indian Ocean, off the northwest coast of the Indonesian island of Sumatra. The resulting tsunami took an estimated 300,000 lives. But there is much more to Southeast Asia than the hazards described in Chapter 3. Tiny Singapore is one of the world's most prosperous nations. It ranks at or near the top among countries in having a positive business climate. Its port and airport are among the world's largest and best. The country's per-capita gross domestic product is comparable to that of most West European countries.

Elsewhere in the region, Indonesia is beginning to industrialize, and the economy of the Philippines continues to grow at a brisk pace. Today, throughout Southeast Asia, a rapid transition is being made from traditional and primary economic activities to a flourishing economy based on manufacturing and services. The region's future appears to be extremely bright.

Tropical Islands

Widely scattered across the vast expanses of the Pacific and Indian oceans are thousands of small islands, some a mere speck rising above the surrounding sea. A few of these islands are prospering, but most remain dirt poor. Nearly all islands experienced colonial status, and a number of them continue to exist as territories. The islands of Guam, Midway, Wake, and American Samoa are politically linked to the United States. With the exception of Hawaii, which is an airline crossroads and destination, most islands are extremely isolated and have few links with the outside world.

8

Tropical Lands in the Twenty-first Century

Writing more than a century ago, Russian geographer and climatologist Alexander Woeikof suggested that tropical lands between 15 degrees north and south latitude could, if necessary, support a population of 10 billion people. Although his view seems a bit optimistic, it may hold some truth. You must remember that the tropical latitudes are the original homeland of humankind. We have lived in this ecosystem throughout our history, and today, fully 10 percent of the human population resides in this realm. Some countries (or, in the case of Indonesia, portions of countries, such as the island of Java) have among the world's highest population densities. Clearly, the natural environment is not the chief obstacle to progress in the Wet Tropics.

The region has many plusses, at least in terms of its potential. If they are healthy, well educated, and free to pursue their goals, humans will always become a country's most important resource. Certainly, the residents of natural-resource-poor lands such as

In recent years, an increasing number of countries within the tropics have become democracies. One such country is Nigeria, which
became a democratic republic in 1999. Pictured here are support-
ers of the Alliance for Democracy Party (AD) during a rally in the
streets of Lagos, shortly before the general elections in 2003.

Singapore, Barbados, and Hawaii have proven this belief to be true time and time again.

Few areas of the tropical realm are without some natural element or combination of elements to which they can turn for development. They may possess good soils, mineral wealth, spectacular scenery, or a combination of these blessings.

What is lacking within much of this region is that essential combination of factors that makes progress possible. First, to reach its potential, a country and people must be well-governed. People must feel safe and secure, and they must be free, within the limits of the law, to pursue their own destinies. Their government must provide educational opportunities for all citizens and adequate health care must be available. It must also develop an adequate infrastructure of transportation, communication, and other public needs. Second, the economic and social systems must be stabilized, and rampant corruption must cease. Investors, whether foreign or domestic, must believe that their capital investments will be safe and secure. Third, and closely related to the first and second points, class, tribal, religious, or other cultural conflicts must be resolved and conditions stabilized. Resolving these problems will be a huge order for many tropical countries.

Historical geography has shown, however, that these seemingly insurmountable obstacles can be overcome, and throughout much of the region, there are signs of progress. Several decades ago, nearly all tropical world countries were struggling. Today, democracy is gaining ground, economies are growing, population growth is declining, and countries are gradually being drawn into the global community. Based on these glimmerings of success, it is possible to look ahead with considerable hope and optimism for continued progress for the world's Wet Tropical lands and peoples.

Historical Geography
at a Glance

< One million YBP*	Humans (*Homo sapiens*) are believed by many scientists to have originated in equatorial eastern Africa.
700,000 YBP	Bones of "Java Man" found on the Indonesian island suggest early migration out of Africa.
32,000 YBP	Earliest evidence suggesting humans may have reached the American tropics. (A great deal of controversy exists with regard to the actual time.)
25,000 YBP	Southeast Asiatic peoples begin island hopping by boat in western Pacific Basin.
600 B.C.	Phoenician navigators sailing under the direction of Egyptian King Necho are believed to have circumnavigated Africa.
200 B.C.	Arab traders may have reached the Spice Islands (present-day Indonesia).
1400s A.D.	European navigators trained in Prince Henry of Portugal's school reach equatorial Africa and beyond.
1492	Christopher Columbus reaches outer Bahamas and settles on north coast of Caribbean island of Hispañola.
1493	Columbus moves settlement to Santo Domingo, on the south shore of Hispañola (Dominican Republic), which becomes oldest permanently settled European community in the New World.

1494 Treaty of Tordesillas divides much of the world between the Spanish (west) and Portuguese (east).

1507 Mapmaker Martin Waldseemüller is first to use "America" on a map; the name possibly is attributed to Columbus, who visited the coast of Nicaragua and learned of gold in the Amerique Mountains.

Sixteenth Century Between 1510 and 1580, Spaniards (and Portuguese in Brazil) lay claim to and settle most of Wet Tropical America.

1511 Portuguese traders reach Indonesia.

1521 Ferdinand Magellan, sailing under the Spanish flag, reaches the Philippines, where he is killed by natives.

1541 Francisco de Orellana, traveling from Andean headwaters to the river's mouth in the Atlantic Ocean, discovers the Amazon River.

1564 The Philippines become a Spanish colony.

1596 Several Dutch ships arrive at a port on the island of Java to take on a cargo of spices.

1602 Dutch drive British and Portuguese from the Spice Islands, and, with the formation of the Dutch East India Company, begin to monopolize the lucrative spice trade.

1795–1806 Scottish explorer Mungo Park travels through portions of tropical Africa.

1804 Haiti gains independence from France to become the world's first black-controlled independent country.

1815 Indonesia's Tambora Volcano erupts with a force believed to have been the greatest in recorded history, causing an estimated 250,000 deaths.

1850–1873 After traveling throughout much of central, southern, and eastern Africa, Scottish explorer David Livingstone becomes ill and loses contact with the outside world for six years; in 1869, a

New York newspaper sends Henry Morton Stanley to Africa in search of the lost explorer.

1871   Henry Morton Stanley discovers David Livingstone in a village on the shores of Lake Tanganyika and utters the now famous statement, "Dr. Livingstone, I presume?"

1883   Krakatoa Volcano, located west of the Indonesian island of Java, erupts violently, taking an estimated 35,000 to 40,000 lives in the immediate area and tens of thousands more with the resulting tsunami.

1913–1965   Dr. Albert Schweitzer, a German-born physician, opens a hospital in Lambaréné, Gabon, which he continues to staff until his death in 1965; for his humanitarian efforts, Schweitzer receives the 1952 Nobel Peace Prize.

1914   Panama Canal opens.

1935   American pilot Jimmy Angel discovers spectacular Angel Falls, which cascades a total of 3,212 feet (979 meters) in two separate stages from a flat-topped tepui near the border of Venezuela and Guyana.

1984   Lake Monoun in Cameroon explodes, resulting in the release of deadly carbon dioxide, which kills nearly 1,800 people.

1999   Panama is given full control of Panama Canal.

2003   An Indonesian reticulated python is captured on the island of Java; it measures 49 feet (15 meters) in length and 2.8 feet (0.85 meters) in diameter, and it weighs 992 pounds (450 kilograms).

2004   Earthquake with magnitude of 9.0 on Richter scale strikes off northwest coast of the Indonesian island of Sumatra; the resulting tsunami kills an estimated 250,000 to 300,000 people.

* years before present

Bibliography

Bates, Marston. *Where Winter Never Comes.* New York: Charles Scribner's Sons, 1952.

de la Rüe, E Aubert. *The Tropics.* New York: Knopf, 1957.

Denevan, William M. "Development and the Imminent Demise of the Amazon Rain Forest." *The Professional Geographer* 25:7 (May 1973): pp. 130–135.

Gourou, Pierre. *The Tropical World: Its Social and Economic Conditions and Its Future Status*, 3rd ed. London: Longmans, Green, 1961.

Jacobs, Marius, R. Kruk, et al., eds. *The Tropical Rain Forest: A First Encounter.* New York: Springer-Verlag, 1988.

Newby, Eric. *The World Atlas of Exploration.* London: Artists House, 1982.

Phillips, Douglas A. *Southeast Asia.* Philadelphia: Chelsea House Publishers, 2006.

Phillips, John. *The Development of Agriculture and Forestry in the Tropics: Patterns, Problems, and Promise.* New York: Praeger, 1961.

Richards, Paul. *The Tropical Rain Forest.* Cambridge: Cambridge University Press, 1952.

Further Reading

Bates, Marston. *Where Winter Never Comes*. New York: Charles Scribner's Sons, 1952.

Christianson, Martha C., ed. *The Emerald Realm: Earth's Precious Rain Forests*. Washington, D.C.: National Geographic Society, 1990.

Collins, W.B. *The Perpetual Forest*. New York: J.B. Lippincott Company, 1959.

dc la Rüe, E Aubert. *The Tropics*. New York: Knopf, 1957.

Denevan, William M. "Development and the Imminent Demise of the Amazon Rain Forest." *The Professional Geographer* 25:7 (May 1973), pp. 130–135.

Draine, Cathie, and Barbara Hall, eds. *Culture Shock: Indonesia*. Portland, Ore.: Graphic Arts Center, 1991.

Einfield, Jann, ed. *Indonesia* (History of Nations). San Diego, Calif.: Greenhaven Press, 2004.

Forbath, Peter. *The River Congo*. New York: E.P. Dutton, 1979.

Gourou, Pierre. *The Tropical World: Its Social and Economic Conditions and Its Future Status*, 3rd ed. London: Longmans, Green, 1961.

Hodder, B.W. *Economic Development in the Tropics*. London: Methuen, 1973.

Jackson, I.J. *Climate, Water and Agriculture in the Tropics*. London and New York: Longman, 1977.

Jacobs, Marius. *The Tropical Rain Forest: A First Encounter*. New York: Springer-Verlag, 1988.

Kelly, Brian, and Mark London. *Amazon*. San Diego: Harcourt Brace Jovanovich Publishers, 1983.

Newby, Eric. *The World Atlas of Exploration.* London: Artists House, 1982.

Phillips, John. *The Development of Agriculture and Forestry in the Tropics: Patterns, Problems, and Promise.* New York: Praeger, 1961.

Place, Susan E., ed. *Tropical Rainforests: Latin American Nature and Society in Transition.* Wilmington, Del.: A Scholarly Resources Inc. Imprint, 1993.

Richards, Paul. *The Tropical Rain Forest.* Cambridge: Cambridge University Press, 1952.

Stewart, Douglas Ian. *Living on the Transamazon Highway After the Trees.* Austin: University of Texas Press, 1994.

Taylor, Jean Gelman. *Indonesia: Peoples and Histories.* New Haven, Conn.: Yale University Press, 2003.

Turnbull, Colin M. *The Forest People: A Study of the Pygmies of the Congo.* New York: Simon and Schuster, 1962.

Wagley, Charles, ed. *Man in the Amazon.* Gainesville: The University Presses of Florida, 1974.

SELECTED CHELSEA HOUSE BOOKS OF INTEREST

Greenbaum, Harry. *Brazil,* 2003.

Mildenstein, Tammy, and Samuel C. Stiers, *The Philippines,* 2004.

Oppong, Joseph R. *The Democratic Republic of the Congo,* 2007.

———, and Esther D. Oppong, *Ghana,* 2003.

Phillips, Douglas A. *Indonesia,* 2004.

———, *Nigeria,* 2003.

———, *Southeast Asia,* 2006.

WEB SITES

The World Factbook
http://www.cia.gov/cia/publications/factbook/index.html

The Amazon Rain Forest
http://www.mre.gov.br/cdbrasil/itamaraty/web/ingles/meioamb/ecossist/amazon/

The Humid Tropics
   http://www.unu.edu/unupress/unupbooks/uu27se/uu27se04.htm

Geography 101: Tropical Rain Forests
   http://www.uwsp.edu/geo/faculty/ritter/geog101/uwsp_lectures/climates_tropical_rain forest.html

Picture Credits

Index

About the Author

CHARLES F. GRITZNER is distinguished professor of geography at South Dakota State University in Brookings. He is now in his fifth decade of teaching at the college level, conducting scholarly research, and writing. In addition to teaching, he enjoys traveling, writing, working with teachers, and sharing his love of geography with classroom students and readers alike. As series editor and frequent author for Chelsea House's MODERN WORLD NATIONS and MODERN WORLD CULTURES series, and now author of the three-volume series GEOGRAPHY OF EXTREME ENVIRONMENTS, he has a wonderful opportunity to combine each of these "hobbies."

Professionally, Gritzner has served as both president and executive director of the National Council for Geographic Education. He has received numerous awards in recognition of his academic and teaching achievements, including the NCGE's George J. Miller Award for Distinguished Service to geography and geographic education, the Association of American Geographers Award for Excellence in Teaching, and the Gilbert Grosvenor Honors in Geographic Education.